I  MY
SLOW
COOKER

I ♥ MY SLOW COOKER

MORE THAN 100
OF THE BEST EVER RECIPES

BEVERLY LeBLANC

NOURISH
EAT WELL, LIVE WELL

I Love My Slow Cooker
Beverly LeBlanc

This edition published in the United Kingdom and Ireland in 2015
by Nourish, an imprint of Watkins Media Limited
19 Cecil Court
London WC2N 4EZ

enquiries@nourishbooks.com

Managing Editor: Grace Cheetham
Editors: Krissy Mallett and Jo Murray
Managing Designer: Manisha Patel
Design and photography art direction: Paul Reid at cobalt id
Production: Uzma Taj
Commissioned photography: William Lingwood
Food Stylist: Lucy Mckelvie
Prop Stylist: Liz Hippisley

A CIP record for this book is available from the
British Library

ISBN: 978-1-84899-037-1

10

Typeset in Adobe Garamond Pro and Calibri
Colour reproduction by Colourscan
Printed in China

To PMOB

Vegetarian Recipes
Vegetarian recipes in this book contain no meat, poultry,
game, fish or shellfish. They may include eggs or cheese.
Cheese, especially those made using traditional methods,
may contain calf rennet, so check labels first. Look for
'suitable for vegetarians', the 'V' sign or 'contains vegetarian
rennet' on the label.

Notes on the recipes
Unless otherwise stated:
All the recipes serve 4
All recipes have been tested in a 3.5l/122fl oz/13½-cup
  oval slow cooker
Use medium eggs, fruit and vegetables
Use fresh ingredients, including herbs and spices
Do not mix metric and imperial measurements
1 tsp = 5ml 1 tbsp = 15ml 1 cup = 250ml

Author's Acknowledgments
Thank you to all the team at Nourish – especially Grace
Cheetham, Krissy Mallett and Jo Murray – for the care and
attention put into this book. As always, you were a pleasure
to work with.
  Big thank yous and much appreciation also go to my recipe
testers – Philip Back, Philip Clarke, Christa Langan and Veronica
Martell – to Carl Cullingford, Jean Herbert, Maggi Gordon,
Rita Kandela and Janet Podolak (and their families and friends)
for their helpful suggestions and ideas, and to the butchers
at Macken Brothers, Chiswick, London.

nourishbooks.com

CONTENTS

INTRODUCTION

I only developed my appreciation of the benefits of slow-cooker cooking relatively late in my culinary career. And, like any new convert, I want to share my enthusiasm.

Slow cookers are simple electrical appliances which, as the name implies, slowly cook food with indirect low-heat transfer in a moist environment. The temperature inside the pot builds up slowly and then remains constant, so slow cookers are especially good at cooking one-pot favourites like casseroles, curries, soups, stews and tagines. They are also versatile enough to cook pot roasts, poultry, roasts, rice and many desserts.

Slow cookers were first developed in the United States in the 1960s, where they were used to cook beans on an industrial scale. In the 1970s, they were embraced by the domestic market as more women entered the workforce. Later, as microwaves and ready-meals became commonplace, slow cookers fell from favour and developed a bad reputation for producing flavourless, mushy food.

Today, however, slow cookers are enjoying a revival. They are back in pride of place on kitchen counters, as people with busy and unpredictable lifestyles appreciate how versatile the slow cooker is at producing wholesome meals. If you only remember the insipid slow-cooker dishes of the past you are in for a treat as you work your way through this collection of recipes inspired by cuisines from around the world.

The outstanding feature that makes slow cookers such an important part of contemporary kitchens, however, is that once you push the button to start the cooking process, most recipes require no more attention until just before serving. Because there isn't any danger of ingredients catching or burning on the bottom, you don't have to constantly stir, or monitor the progress. It's a great comfort to leave the house in the morning confident that a delicious, satisfying evening meal will be waiting for you when you return. If you invest in a modern model with a programmable timer, you don't even have to worry about dinner overcooking and spoiling if you are delayed, as the slow cooker will automatically switch itself to a WARM setting (see page 9).

Slow cookers can also help stretch your budget on two fronts. The moist, slow cooking process is excellent for tenderizing inexpensive cuts of meat, an important consideration for anyone wanting to cut their food bills. The cookers are also more economical to run than other conventional cooking methods, such as casseroling on the hob or in the oven. Almost all manufacturers make the claim that leaving a slow cooker to cook all day is no more expensive than leaving a light on.

HOW DOES THE SLOW COOKER WORK?
Most slow cookers have the same basic design – a dishwasher-safe stoneware insert, called the 'container' or 'crock', which sits inside a thin metal casing that houses the electrical element, and

a lid. As the condensation accumulates inside the slow cooker it creates a low-pressure seal between the lid and the container. You can observe this when cooking after a long period of time, as water sputters around the edge of the lid. The electrical elements are encased in the side as well as the base, providing all-round heat.

WHICH SLOW COOKER TO BUY?

You have to do your research carefully before buying, as there are many brands and most vary from each other in a variety of ways. There are no industry standards; consequently, slow cookers cook at different temperatures, come in many sizes and can be round or oval.

You also have a wide choice of colours and decorative features. If you like entertaining often, you will even find models that do double duty as a hostess trolley, with space for keeping up to three dishes warm.

Yet, aesthetics are not the primary consideration when buying a slow cooker. The number of people you cook for and the type of food you like eating should ultimately determine which slow cooker you buy. The below chart lists some of the sizes available and their different capabilities.

WHICH SLOW COOKER TO BUY?

SIZE	SERVES	ROUND	OVAL
1.5l/52fl oz/ 6 cups	1–2	Casseroles and stews, soups, single lamb shanks, stewed fruit, compotes, half quantities of most of the recipes in this book	
3.5l/122fl oz/13½ cups	4–6	Casseroles and stews, soups, 4 lamb shanks, small gammon joints, stewed fruit, compotes, desserts cooked in round containers up to 1l/35fl oz/4 cups, whole quantities of all the recipes in this book except whole chickens and some joints of meat	Casseroles and stews, soups, 4 lamb shanks, small gammon joints, stewed fruit, compotes, desserts cooked in round containers up to 1l/35fl oz/4 cups, small chickens and joints of meat, desserts cooked in a 450g/1lb loaf tin, whole quantities of all the recipes in this book
4.7l/165fl oz/ 19 cups	6–8	Casseroles and stews, soups, 4 lamb shanks, small gammon joints, stewed fruit, compotes, desserts cooked in round containers up to 1l/35fl oz/4 cups, whole quantities of all the recipes in this book	Casseroles and stews, soups, 4 lamb shanks, small gammon joints, stewed fruit, compotes, desserts cooked in round containers up to 1l/35fl oz/4 cups, small and medium chickens, joints of meat, desserts cooked in a 450g/1lb loaf tin, whole quantities of all the recipes in this book
6l/210fl oz/ 24 cups	8+	Casseroles and stews, soups, 6 lamb shanks, gammon joints, stewed fruit, compotes, desserts cooked in round containers up to 1.25l/44fl oz/5 cups, medium poultry and joints of meat, if they are rolled, whole quantities of all the recipes in this book, double quantities of the curry, casserole and stew recipes	Casseroles and stews, soups, 6 lamb shanks, small gammon joints, stewed fruit, compotes, desserts cooked in round containers up to 1.25l/44fl oz/5 cups, most poultry and joints of meat, desserts cooked in a 450g/1lb loaf tin, whole quantities of all the recipes in this book, double quantities of the curry, casserole, soup and stew recipes

As a general rule, the more modern a slow cooker is, the faster it will cook. Consequently, if you're using a slow cooker that's several years old to make the recipes in this book, you will need to adjust the cooking times accordingly.

Which features to look for? Once you have decided what size and shape slow cooker is most suitable for your requirements, there are other options to consider before buying. One way to research is to look at manufacturers' websites to compare models and features. This will also give you access to many users' manuals, some of which specify temperatures for different settings, but unfortunately, not always.

Manual or digital slow cooker? The most basic slow cookers have an On/Off switch and HIGH and LOW settings that you select manually. Some models also include an AUTO setting that cooks food on HIGH for one hour before automatically switching the temperature to LOW. Manual slow cookers are an economical option for anyone who is at home all the time and able to monitor the cooking process.

Slightly more expensive digital models, however, give you substantially more flexibility with programmable timings. If, for example, you aren't ready to eat when the cooking is complete, most digital models automatically switch to WARM, keeping the food hot until required. I think this is the most important feature, and essential for anyone who wants to put the ingredients in the cooker in the morning and come home to a warm meal that hasn't been overcooked into mush. The WARM function is also ideal for households where not everyone is eating at the same time, and can be used to keep some conventionally cooked foods, such as soups and stews, warm until it is time to serve. The WARM setting, however, should never be used to cook food.

Some digital slow cookers also have a SIMMER function, with a temperature that sits between LOW and WARM, for simmering soups.

The most sophisticated digital slow cookers come with a digital probe and are particularly good for cooking poultry and large joints. These models cook according to temperature, rather than time, automatically switching to WARM when a specified internal temperature is reached.

Be sure to check how much flexibility a specific model offers before buying. My favourite slow cooker, for example, allows me to set the HIGH or LOW settings for up to 24 hours, and the WARM function keeps food hot for 8 hours, while other models have shorter settings.

Digital slow cookers also have an LCD display panel that counts down so you can see at a glance how much cooking time is left.

Is preheating required? Some manufacturers specify to preheat the empty slow cooker for 20 minutes before adding any ingredients. Think about if this will be convenient for you or not. Many of the recipes in this book don't specify preheating because they were tested in a slow cooker that doesn't require it, but consult your slow cooker's manual before using any of the recipes and preheat the cooker if required.

Glass lids Although not essential, I favour a see-through lid, rather than a solid ceramic one, so that I am able to monitor how the condensation is building up in the container. Because slow cookers make very little noise and give off fewer aromas than other methods of cooking, it can be reassuring to confirm by sight that the dish is progressing.

From cooker to table The early generation of slow cookers did not have removable porcelain, ceramic or dishwasher-safe containers, but this is a standard feature of modern cookers. To reduce the amount of washing up, buy a slow cooker with a container you are happy to serve from at the table.

The containers become very hot, so make sure the handles on the sides are large enough for you to easily lift it out of the metal casing. You will need to use oven gloves or a folded tea towel when you remove it, and you'll need a heatproof mat to put the hot container on.

Some larger models come with heatproof containers that are also safe to use on the hob, which is another way to save on the washing up.

Portability If you take meals to the elderly or ill, or just like sharing food with friends, consider one of the slow cooker models which comes with a securely locking lid so you can transport the container without spillages. Some models also have insulated bags for transporting the slow cooker with hot food inside, so it arrives hot and ready to eat.

Long leads This is a minor but important point to consider. Think about where the electrical socket you will be using is located and make sure the slow cooker has a long enough lead. As with all electrical appliances, the lead should not be near gas or electric rings on the hob, nor should it be too close to the sink. The outside of a slow cooker becomes very hot, so place it out of reach of small children and somewhere you are unlikely to burn yourself.

HOW TO USE YOUR SLOW COOKER

Cooking in a slow cooker is both similar to and different from conventional cooking. The significant change required to your cooking technique is not to lift the lid before the end of the specified cooking time, unless instructed to in a recipe. Lifting the lid breaks the seal and lowers the temperature. Getting used to not lifting the lid is challenging when first using a slow cooker, as a cook's natural inclination is to sniff, stir and taste, but you must resist. If you do lift the lid, however, add 15 minutes to the total cooking time.

Although slow cookers don't require much attention once you switch them on, a certain amount of pre-cooking preparation is necessary, and this can take as much time as if you are

preparing, say, a stew on the hob. I think it is a misconception about cooking in a slow cooker that you always just throw all the ingredients in, switch it on and walk out the door. Although some recipes follow that brief – and I've included a selection of them in this book – but for the best results, the majority require your attention to get them started.

Since the heat in a slow cooker builds up from the bottom, put the densest ingredients, such as chopped root vegetables, in the cooker first and then add the meat and liquids.

If, like me, you aren't really interested in cooking your evening meal while eating breakfast, there are several techniques to get around this problem. Sometimes I cook really slow-cooking recipes, like Tuscan Lamb Shanks & Butter Beans (see page 77), overnight and transfer them to a conventional casserole or saucepan in the morning, ready for reheating that evening. More often, however, I do all the chopping and initial frying the night before so in the morning I really can put everything in the slow cooker, switch it on and walk out the door.

The most basic guideline of conventional cooking, however, also applies to cooking in a slow cooker: what you put in a slow cooker determines what you get out. Even though slow cookers are adept at transforming tough, inexpensive cuts of meat into tender meals, that doesn't mean you can use poor-quality ingredients and expect a good outcome. Always use good-quality meat, seafood and fruit and vegetables for the most satisfying results.

Adding liquids Many old-fashioned slow-cooker recipes specify to cover all the ingredients with liquid before covering with the lid and beginning the cooking process, but this isn't necessary. Recipes cooked in a slow cooker require *much* less liquid than those cooked on the hob or in the oven, because less evaporation takes place. This means the liquid that cooks out of any ingredients stays in the container. It is this liquid and any added liquid that creates the condensation, and if you have a glass lid you will see this building up and dropping from the lid back down onto the ingredients. Resist the temptation to add more liquid than specified in recipes until you are familiar with how your slow cooker operates.

You'll see many of the recipes in this book specify very small amounts of liquid. In Greek Spiced Beef & Onion Stew (see page 82), for example, the cubes of stewing beef cook in just the liquid from 450g/1lb grated tomatoes, 4 tablespoons of dissolved tomato purée and 2 tablespoons of red wine vinegar to produce a rich, thick stew.

Boosting the flavours Because of the condensation that collects in the slow cooker, flavours actually become diluted, not concentrated as you will often read. You need to add more herbs and spices than in conventional cooking to avoid insipid food. If your favourite conventional casserole recipe, for example, includes 1 crushed garlic clove, think about using 2–4 if you cook it in a slow cooker. I appreciate that sounds like an overpowering amount, but after a stew has simmered for eight hours the flavours will have mellowed.

Dried herbs, rather than fresh, are used in most slow-cooker recipes because the fresh ones simply lose their potency after long, slow cooking. Add fresh herbs at the end or sprinkled over the finished dish when their flavours will be appreciated. Some recipes specify to add dried herbs loose and these will be present in the finished dish, while a few specify to tie them in a piece of muslin so they can be removed at the end of cooking.

Cooking poultry Whole chicken and poultry portions cook quickly and easily in slow cookers. To avoid any possibility of salmonella poisoning, my recipes specify to cook chicken and turkey dishes quickly on the HIGH setting. I also suggest you don't leave cooked poultry dishes for a long time on the WARM setting.

Chicken skin can be given an appetizing golden colour by browning it before adding to the slow cooker but it will lose its crispness. If you find this unappealing, remove the skin from the chicken before you add the pieces to the container.

Cooking beans and pulses Dried and soaked beans and pulses should be covered with liquid while they cook. If necessary, add extra boiling stock or liquid before you switch the slow cooker on so they are just submerged. It isn't necessary for drained and rinsed tinned beans and pulses to be covered with liquid.

Cooking rice Easy-cook white or brown rice is the best choice for cooking in a slow cooker. This rice has been parboiled and gives you tender, separate grains when cooked in a slow cooker. If you try other ordinary long-grain rice it becomes too sticky to be enjoyable. The Pumpkin & Dolcelatte Rice recipe (see page 132), however, uses risotto rice because the desired result is thicker and creamier than many rice recipes.

Cooking vegetables The long, slow cooking process in a slow cooker is ideal for cooking root vegetables as it brings out their natural sweetness. It is important, however, to cut vegetables to similar sizes so they cook uniformly. Because vegetables are generally put in the bottom of the cooker, they are usually sufficiently covered with liquid but this isn't always necessary. Recipes will specify if you should add extra liquid to ensure the vegetables are completely submerged.

Green vegetables, such as pak choi, kale and spinach leaves, are generally added at the end of cooking, to preserve both their texture and their flavour.

Always thaw frozen vegetables, such as peas, before adding them to the slow cooker. If you are adding tinned vegetables, such as sweetcorn kernels, drain and rinse them well before adding.

Making stocks After the first time I made chicken stock in my slow cooker, it was obvious to me I probably wouldn't be making it again in the conventional manner. I simply put all the ingredients in the cooker before I went to bed and switched the cooker on. In the morning I had a container full of delicious stock, ready for cooling and freezing. Nothing could have been easier. I always think that when I go to the trouble of making stock I might as well make more than I need, so I always have a good frozen supply. All of the stock recipes in this book (see pages 168–169) are ready to use as soon as they have finished cooking, or they can be left to cool completely and then chilled for up to two days, or frozen for up to three months. The exception is the fish stock, which should be used within a day.

Frying ingredients Some recipes specify to fry ingredients before adding them to the slow cooker. This is to give meat a good colour, start the cooking process for vegetables and enhance the flavour of alliums, such as garlic and onions. Also, raw spices such as ground coriander and cumin, need to be fried briefly to cook out the 'raw' flavour. Even if a dish cooks for eight or ten hours in a slow cooker, spices will still taste 'raw' if they aren't fried first.

Many cooks prefer to cut the preparation time by not frying meat before adding it to the cooker. I usually find the texture at the end of cooking, however, less appetizing, although several of my recipes do skip this step and manage to work well. Be sure to pat meat dry before frying, and cook in batches, if necessary, to avoid overcrowding the pan. When the pan is too full, the temperature drops and the meat steams, rather than fries. Browning fatty ingredients, such as chorizo, before adding to the slow cooker helps to eliminate excessive fat from the finished dish.

Covering food during cooking Because of the condensation that builds up and then drips down off the lid, it is necessary to cover certain dishes with foil or cling film while they cook, especially desserts, to prevent them becoming soggy. Cover tightly with cling film or foil, moulded over the top of the dish. When you are cooking something surrounded by boiling water, such as Almond Crème Caramel (see page 159), be sure not to let the cling film or foil extend down to the water level, or steam will seep underneath.

Skimming fat To make the finished dish more appetizing, I think it's important to skim fat from the surface of dishes when they finish cooking, especially when they are made with fatty meat cuts, such as belly pork, chorizo or lamb shanks.

Thickening cooking juices Again, because of the condensation in the slow cooker, sauces tend to be very thin and watery. Recipes compensate for this by using much less liquid than in conventional recipes (see page 10) but there are additional ways to create richer, thicker sauces.

Meat can be dusted with plain flour or cornflour before browning, which will dissolve into the liquid and thicken the juices during the cooking process. Arrowroot or cornflour mixed with a few tablespoons of cold water can be stirred into the slow cooker and then cooked for 15–30 minutes on HIGH until the cooking liquid thickens.

A NOTE ABOUT COOKING TIMES

It is difficult to give accurate cooking times because the cooking temperatures of different brands vary. As a general rule of thumb, older cookers have lower temperatures than modern ones, and smaller cookers cook faster than larger ones.

I also don't give a range of cooking times, but after you've made several of the recipes in this book, you will know if you have to cook for longer or shorter times.

All the recipes in this book have been tested in a 3.5l/122fl oz/13½-cup oval slow cooker with a HIGH temperature of 100°C/212°F and a LOW temperature of 93°C/199°F. Consult your users' manual to see if your cooker's specifications differ, and compare the cooking time in similar recipes to determine if you should cook recipes for longer or shorter times. It is, unfortunately, a matter of trial and error.

If you've lost the users' manual that came with your slow cooker, use this simple test to determine if it is hotter or cooler than the one used for recipe testing. Measure 1l/35fl oz/4 cups water into a large measuring jug and leave to sit on the counter for several hours so it comes to room temperature. Pour it into the slow cooker, cover and switch to HIGH. The water in the test cooker boils after 1½ hours.

THE BEST MEATS TO USE

As with casseroles cooked in the conventional way, the least expensive cuts of meat with tough connective tissues are ideal for using in slow cookers. The slow cooking process breaks down the tissues for tender results. I like to make casseroles and stews with large 5cm/2in pieces of meat. The chart below lists the best cuts of meat for slow cookers.

ENJOY YOUR SLOW COOKER

My conversion to the benefits of using a slow cooker happened one afternoon while I was sitting on a bus stuck in a traffic jam and a beef stew was simmering away at home. It was with a sense of relief that I realized dinner would not be ruined, regardless of how late I was getting home. I knew my slow cooker would automatically switch itself to its WARM setting at the end of the programmed cooking time.

It was, however, a rocky road to conversion. The first recipes I tried were insipid and bland. I regularly complained about eating 'food without soul'. It wasn't until I decided to tear up the rule book and develop my own recipes that I started to really enjoy slow-cooker meals. This collection of recipes is the result of my trials and errors. I made many common mistakes, like adding too much liquid or not enough flavourings, but as I tried and tested, I developed recipes with rich, succulent flavours.

I have tried to push the boundaries of a slow cooker book to give you recipes that are more than just home-comfort meals, but ones that you could make for friends coming round for dinner or for special occasions.

Each recipe shows the time it takes to cook, and a star symbol on some of the recipes indicates whether it's a super-easy meal. Whatever the occasion you'll find everything you ever wanted in this book, and more, for your much-loved slow cooker.

THE BEST CUTS OF MEAT TO USE

Beef	brisket, bone-in short ribs, boneless chuck (shoulder), boneless leg, flank steak, minced beef, ox cheeks, oxtail, shin, silverside, skirt steak
Lamb	boneless leg, boneless shoulder, shank
Pork	belly of pork, boneless leg, boneless pork steaks, boneless shoulder, gammon hock, gammon knuckle, sausages
Veal	boneless shoulder, osso buco (cross-cut shank)

All the recipes in this book have been tested in a 3.5l/122fl oz/13½-cup oval slow cooker with a HIGH temperature of 100°C/212°F and a LOW temperature of 93°C/199°F.

You'll find this symbol whenever a recipe is super-easy to make. This means that there is minimal or no prepping involved. You just add the ingredients and switch on the slow cooker.

SOUPS & SAUCES

The most difficult part about writing this chapter was choosing the recipes to include. The list was long, because a slow cooker is ideal for making soups and sauces: they don't require any attention while they cook and it's virtually impossible for them to scorch and burn. That's a real bonus with the sauce recipes, especially one like Barbecue Sauce (see page 33), with its high sugar content.

I also particularly appreciated the versatility of my slow cooker when I was testing soup recipes at the height of a heat wave and the kitchen wasn't full of steam – it really is a kitchen appliance for the whole year round.

This chapter contains a selection of quick-cooking soups, such as Chicken, Vegetable & Barley Broth (see page 16), as well as soups you can put on in the morning in anticipation of your evening meal. If you want a pot of warming soup waiting for you when you walk through the door after a hard day, try German Lentil Soup (see page 22). Vegetarians will also find a good selection of suitable recipes in this chapter such as the Split Pea, Celeriac & Spinach Soup (see page 23) and the Red Lentil & Sweet Potato Soup (see page 27).

When I go to the effort of making a home-made sauce, I can't see the point of making enough for just one meal. I love using my slow cooker for making hassle-free sauces in larger quantities, so I always have a supply in the freezer. And, again, because the pot doesn't dry out, I just go about my day's activities without giving the simmering sauce a second thought.

◄ CHINESE HOTPOT (SEE PAGE 27)

CHICKEN, VEGETABLE & BARLEY BROTH

PREPARATION TIME: 20 minutes, plus making the stock (optional)
COOKING TIME: 2½ hours on HIGH   **SERVES 4**

350g/12oz mixed root vegetables, such as carrot, celeriac, parsnip, swede and turnip, diced

1 celery stick, thinly sliced

1 leek, halved lengthways, thinly sliced and rinsed

2 bay leaves, tied together with 1 small bunch of parsley sprigs with crushed stalks

2 chicken quarters, skin removed

2 tbsp pot barley

1l/35fl oz/4 cups Chicken Stock (see page 168) or ready-made stock, boiling, plus extra if needed

salt and freshly ground black pepper

snipped chives or chopped parsley leaves, to serve

Put the root vegetables, celery, leek and herb bundle in the slow cooker. Add the chicken quarters and barley, tucking the barley down between the chicken pieces. Pour over the stock, adding extra to cover the barley, if necessary, and season with salt and pepper.

Cover the cooker with the lid. Cook on HIGH for 2 hours until the juices from the chicken run clear when the thickest part of the meat is pierced with the tip of a sharp knife or skewer. Remove the chicken from the cooker and leave to rest for about 10 minutes. Meanwhile, re-cover the cooker and cook for a further 30 minutes until the vegetables and barley are tender.

When the chicken is cool enough to handle, remove the meat from the bones and cut into bite-sized pieces. Wrap in foil and keep warm.

When the vegetables and barley are tender, return the chicken to the cooker and heat through, if necessary. Remove and discard the herb bundle and add a little more salt and pepper, if you like. Sprinkle with chives and serve.

TURKEY, WILD RICE & TOMATO SOUP

PREPARATION TIME: 20 minutes, plus making the stock (optional)
COOKING TIME: 2 hours on HIGH   **SERVES 4**

400g/14oz boneless, skinless turkey breast

turkey bones (optional)

1 tbsp dried basil or dried tarragon

100g/3½oz/heaped ½ cup wild rice

1 tbsp sunflower oil

1 onion, finely chopped

2 garlic cloves, finely chopped

750ml/26fl oz/3 cups Vegetable Stock (see page 169), Chicken Stock (see page 168) or ready-made stock

310ml/10¾fl oz/1¼ cups passata

salt and freshly ground black pepper

shredded basil leaves or chopped tarragon leaves, to serve

crusty bread, to serve (optional)

Season the turkey breast with salt and pepper. Put the turkey in the slow cooker with any bones, if using, and sprinkle over the dried basil. Add the rice, tucking it down around the meat.

Heat the oil in a large frying pan over a high heat. Reduce the heat to medium, add the onion and fry, stirring, for 2 minutes. Add the garlic and fry for a further 1–3 minutes until the onion is softened.

Add the stock and passata and season lightly with salt and pepper. Bring to the boil, then pour the mixture into the cooker.

Cover the cooker with the lid. Cook on HIGH for 2 hours until the rice is fluffy and tender and the juices from the turkey run clear when the thickest part of the meat is pierced with the tip of a sharp knife or skewer. Remove and discard the bones, if necessary. Remove the turkey from the cooker and leave to cool slightly. Re-cover the cooker to keep the rice warm.

When the turkey is cool enough to handle, cut into bite-sized pieces, then return it to the cooker and heat through, if necessary. Add a little more salt and pepper, if you like. Sprinkle with basil and serve with crusty bread, if you like.

VARIATIONS
For a spicier soup, add 1 tablespoon of curry paste with the garlic. The soup is also good with shredded kale. When you remove the turkey, wrap in foil and keep warm, then stir in the kale and cook for 15 minutes on HIGH until it is tender. Return the chopped turkey to the cooker to heat through.

HOT & SOUR DUCK & MUSHROOM SOUP

PREPARATION TIME: 15 minutes, plus making the stock (optional)
COOKING TIME: 3 hours on LOW, plus 20 minutes on HIGH   **SERVES 4**

15g/½oz dried Asian mushrooms, such as oyster or
cloud ear

2 duck legs, about 250g/9oz each, skin
and fat removed

6 Thai shallots or 3 large French shallots, halved

1 dried red Thai chilli, deseeded if you like, and halved

1½ tsp caster sugar

1l/35fl oz/4 cups Vegetable Stock (see page 169)
or water

2 tbsp fish sauce, plus extra to taste

1 tbsp lemon juice, plus extra to taste

1 tbsp arrowroot or cornflour

90g/3¼oz/1 cup bean sprouts

salt and freshly ground black pepper

coriander leaves or Thai basil leaves, to serve

Put the dried mushrooms in a sieve and rinse under cold running water to remove any dirt.

Put the duck legs, mushrooms, shallots, chilli and sugar in the slow cooker. Pour over the stock, fish sauce and lemon juice, stirring to dissolve the sugar. Season with salt and pepper.

Cover the cooker with the lid. Cook on LOW for 3 hours until the juices from the duck run clear when the thickest part of the meat is pierced with the tip of a sharp knife or skewer. Remove the duck from the cooker and leave to rest for about 10 minutes.

Meanwhile, remove the shallots and chilli and discard. Put the arrowroot and 2 tablespoons cold water in a small bowl and stir until smooth, then stir the paste into the cooking liquid. Switch the cooker to HIGH, re-cover and cook for 15 minutes until the soup has thickened slightly.

When the duck is cool enough to handle, remove all the meat from the bones and cut into thin pieces. When the soup has thickened, return the duck to the cooker with the bean sprouts and stir to heat through. Add a little more fish sauce, lemon juice and salt and pepper, if you like. Sprinkle with coriander and serve.

COOK'S TIP
Use a small knife to carefully remove the skin and fat from the duck legs – the legs are slippery and difficult to handle so it helps if you dust your fingers with salt first.

GERMAN LENTIL SOUP

If you've never added a splash of vinegar to a bowlful of lentil soup, give it a try.
Stirring in as little as half a teaspoon per serving really lifts the flavour.

PREPARATION TIME: 15 minutes
COOKING TIME: 6 hours on LOW, plus 30 minutes on HIGH   **SERVES 4**

1 tbsp sunflower oil, plus extra if needed

85g/3oz smoked lardons or thick smoked back bacon, sliced

2 carrots, diced

1 onion, finely chopped

½ celery stick, finely chopped

200g/7oz/heaped 1 cup brown lentils, rinsed

1 floury potato, such as Desiree, King Edward and Maris Piper, about 200g/7oz, chopped

2 bay leaves

1 tbsp dried parsley

1 tbsp dried thyme

4 smoked or plain frankfurters, cut into bite-sized pieces

salt and freshly ground black pepper

2 tsp red wine vinegar or white wine vinegar or to taste, to serve

chopped parsley leaves, to serve

dark rye bread (optional), to serve

Heat the oil in a large frying pan over a high heat. Reduce the heat to low, add the lardons and fry for 1–2 minutes until they give off their fat and start to crisp. Use a slotted spoon to transfer the lardons to the slow cooker.

Add the carrots, onion and celery to the pan, adding extra oil if necessary, and fry, stirring, for 3–5 minutes until the onion is softened. Transfer the vegetables to the cooker, then add the lentils, potato, bay leaves, dried parsley and thyme and season with pepper. Pour over 1l/35fl oz/4 cups boiling water, or enough to cover the lentils.

Cover the cooker with the lid and cook on LOW for 6 hours until the lentils and potato are almost tender. Remove and discard the bay leaves. Season with salt and a little more pepper, if you like, and stir in the frankfurters.

Switch the cooker to HIGH, re-cover and cook for 30 minutes until the frankfurters are hot. Stir in the vinegar, sprinkle with parsley and serve with dark rye bread, if you like.

SPLIT PEA, CELERIAC & SPINACH SOUP

PREPARATION TIME: 20 minutes, plus making the stock (optional)
COOKING TIME: 5 hours 20 minutes on HIGH **SERVES 4**

280g/10oz/1¼ cups green split peas, rinsed

100g/3½oz celeriac, peeled and diced

2 garlic cloves, chopped

1 bay leaf

1 onion, chopped

1.2l/40fl oz/4¾ cups Vegetable Stock (see page 169), Chicken Stock (see page 168) or ready-made stock, boiling, plus extra if needed

1 tbsp white wine vinegar

200g/7oz baby spinach leaves

4 smoked bacon or cured streaky bacon rashers (optional)

salt and freshly ground black pepper

finely chopped dill or parsley leaves, to serve

Put the split peas, celeriac, garlic, bay leaf and onion in the slow cooker. Pour over the stock, adding extra to cover the split peas, if necessary, and season with pepper.

Cover the cooker with the lid and cook on HIGH for 5 hours until the split peas are dissolving and the celeriac is very tender. Stir in the vinegar and add the spinach, using a spoon to push it into the soup. Cook, uncovered, for a further 10–15 minutes, stirring once, until the spinach is tender. Season with salt and a little more pepper, if you like.

Strain the soup, reserving the cooking liquid. Remove and discard the bay leaf. Purée the split peas, celeriac and spinach in a blender or food processor until smooth, then return the mixture to the cooker and slowly stir in the reserved liquid until the desired consistency is achieved. Re-cover the cooker to keep the soup warm.

Meanwhile, for the bacon, if using, preheat the grill to high. When hot, grill the bacon for 2–3 minutes on each side until cooked and crisp. Drain well on kitchen paper, then finely chop. Sprinkle the soup with the bacon and dill and serve.

VARIATION
For a vegetarian version, omit the bacon and sprinkle the soup with toasted pumpkin or sunflower seeds for texture and crumbled feta cheese for richness.

SMOKY & SPICY BLACK BEAN SOUP

PREPARATION TIME: 30 minutes, plus making the stock and tortilla chips (optional)
COOKING TIME: 10 hours on LOW **SERVES 4**

2 tbsp olive oil

100g/3½oz smoked lardons

1 large onion, finely chopped

4 large garlic cloves, finely chopped

1 tbsp ground cumin

2 tsp ground coriander

½ tsp ground cloves

¼ tsp cayenne pepper

800ml/28fl oz/scant 3½ cups Chicken Stock (see page 168), Vegetable Stock (see page 169) or ready-made stock, plus extra if needed

250g/9oz/scant 1¼ cups dried black beans

2 tbsp dried oregano

1 tbsp dried thyme

1 dried chipotle chilli pepper, deseeded if you like

1 avocado

1 tbsp lime juice

salt and freshly ground black pepper

feta cheese, drained and crumbled, to serve

cherry tomatoes, deseeded and chopped

chopped coriander leaves, to serve

lime wedges, to serve

Tortilla Chips (see page 174) or shop-bought tortilla chips, to serve

ADDITIONAL TOPPINGS (OPTIONAL)

hard-boiled eggs, shelled and finely chopped

spring onions, finely chopped

soured cream

Heat 1 tablespoon of the oil in a large saucepan over a high heat. Reduce the heat to low, add the lardons and fry for 1–2 minutes until they give off their fat and start to crisp. Use a slotted spoon to transfer the lardons to the slow cooker.

Pour off any excess fat from the pan, leaving about 1 tablespoon. Add the onion and fry, stirring, for 2 minutes. Add the garlic, cumin, ground coriander, cloves and cayenne pepper and fry for a further 1–3 minutes until the onion is softened.

Add the stock, beans, oregano, thyme and chipotle chilli and season with pepper. Bring to the boil and boil vigorously for 10 minutes. Pour the bean mixture into the cooker and add extra stock to just cover the beans, if necessary.

Cover the cooker with the lid and cook on LOW for 10 hours until the beans are very tender. Remove and discard the chipotle chilli.

Transfer half of the beans and liquid to a blender or food processor and purée, or mash in a bowl. Return the mixture to the cooker and stir into the soup. Season with salt and a little more pepper.

Stone, peel and finely chop the avocado, then toss with the lime juice. Divide the soup into bowls, top with the avocado, feta cheese and tomatoes and sprinkle with coriander. Serve with lime wedges for squeezing over, tortilla chips and a selection of additional toppings, if you like.

CHINESE HOTPOT

PREPARATION TIME: 10 minutes,
 plus making the stock (optional)
COOKING TIME: 9½ hours on LOW,
 plus 30 minutes on HIGH   **SERVES 4**

500g/1lb 2oz beef flank
600ml/21fl oz/scant 2½ cups Beef Stock
 (see page 168) or ready-made stock
125ml/4fl oz/½ cup Chinese rice wine
3 garlic cloves, crushed
1 star anise
2 tsp chilli bean paste
2 tsp caster sugar
1½ tsp ground cumin
1 tbsp soy sauce
a pinch of Szechuan pepper
150g/5½oz thin Chinese egg noodles
2.5cm/1in piece of root ginger
1 tsp toasted sesame oil
4 spring onions, finely chopped, to serve
chopped coriander leaves, to serve

Put the beef, stock, rice wine, garlic, star anise,
chilli bean paste, sugar, cumin, soy sauce and
Szechuan pepper in the slow cooker, stirring
to dissolve the chilli bean paste.

Cover the cooker and cook on LOW for 9½ hours
until the beef is very tender. Remove the beef
from the cooker, wrap in foil and leave to rest for
10 minutes. Meanwhile, switch the cooker to HIGH,
re-cover and cook for 15 minutes. Stir in the
noodles, re-cover and cook for a further 15 minutes
until they are tender.

Shred the beef, then re-wrap and keep warm.
When the noodles are cooked, stir in the beef,
then grate the ginger directly into the broth and
add the sesame oil. Sprinkle with spring onions and
coriander and serve.

RED LENTIL & SWEET POTATO SOUP

PREPARATION TIME: 15 minutes,
 plus making the stock (optional)
COOKING TIME: 3 hours on HIGH   **SERVES 4**

1 large red onion, finely chopped
4 large garlic cloves, finely chopped
a pinch of dried chilli flakes
1 sweet potato, about 250g/9oz, diced
1 red pepper, halved lengthways, deseeded and
 quartered
150g/5½oz/¾ cup red lentils, rinsed
1l/35fl oz/4 cups Vegetable Stock (see page 169)
 or ready-made stock, boiling, plus extra if needed
1 tbsp olive oil
2 tsp balsamic vinegar
salt and freshly ground black pepper
chopped parsley leaves, to serve

Put all the ingredients except the vinegar in the
slow cooker and season with pepper. Add extra
stock to cover the lentils, if necessary.

Cover the cooker with the lid and cook on HIGH
for 3 hours until the lentils and sweet potato are
tender.

Remove the pepper pieces and discard. Stir well
and season with salt and a little more pepper,
if you like. Stir in the vinegar, sprinkle with parsley
and serve.

SUMMER TOMATO SOUP

PREPARATION TIME: 15 minutes, plus making
the stock (optional)
COOKING TIME: 2½ hours on HIGH, plus
5½ hours on LOW **SERVES 4**

4 large garlic cloves, chopped
2 celery sticks, chopped
1 large red onion, chopped
1.4kg/3lb 2oz juicy tomatoes, deseeded and chopped
2 bay leaves
1 tbsp dried parsley
1 tsp caster sugar
125ml/4fl oz/½ cup Vegetable Stock (see page 169)
   or ready-made stock, plus extra if needed
salt and freshly ground black pepper
4 tbsp crème fraîche, to serve

Put the garlic, celery and red onion in the slow
cooker. Add the tomatoes, bay leaves, parsley,
sugar and stock, then season with salt and pepper.

Cover the cooker with the lid and cook on HIGH
for 2½ hours. Stir the tomatoes well. Switch the
cooker to LOW, re-cover and cook for a further
5½ hours until the tomatoes have broken down and
the vegetables are tender. Remove and discard the
bay leaves.

Strain the soup into a bowl, pressing down to extract
as much liquid as possible. Reserve the cooking
liquid. Purée the tomato mixture in a blender or
food processor until smooth, then return the mixture
to the cooker and slowly stir in the reserved cooking
liquid and extra stock, if necessary, until the desired
consistency is achieved. Add a little more salt and
pepper, if you like. Serve hot or chilled, with a dollop
of crème fraîche.

SPICED SQUASH & APPLE SOUP

PREPARATION TIME: 15 minutes, plus making
the stock and cream (optional)
COOKING TIME: 12 hours on LOW   **SERVES 4**

450g/1lb butternut squash, peeled, deseeded and cut
   into 1cm/½in pieces
2.5cm/1in piece of root ginger, peeled and chopped
2 bay leaves, torn
2 cinnamon sticks
2 large garlic cloves, finely chopped
1 Granny Smith apple, peeled, cored and chopped
1 leek, halved lengthways, finely chopped and rinsed
1 tsp ground coriander
⅛ tsp cayenne pepper, or to taste
1l/35fl oz/4 cups Vegetable Stock (see page 169)
   or ready-made stock
2 tbsp apple juice
salt and freshly ground black pepper
finely chopped parsley leaves, to serve
sunflower seeds, to serve
1 recipe quantity Maple Cream (see page 171),
   to serve (optional)

Put the squash, ginger, bay leaves, cinnamon sticks,
garlic, apple, leek, coriander and cayenne pepper
in the slow cooker. Season with salt and pepper,
then pour over the stock.

Cover the cooker with the lid and cook on LOW for
12 hours until the squash is very tender and the
flavours are blended. Remove and discard the bay
leaves and cinnamon sticks. Purée the soup in a
blender or food processor until smooth. Stir in the
apple juice and add a little more salt and pepper, if
you like. Sprinkle with parsley and sunflower seeds
and serve with a swirl of Maple Cream, if you like.

MINESTRONE

This soup is full of fresh Mediterranean flavours. You can make it in advance and reheat it, but only add the thin pasta pieces just before serving – they become overcooked and mushy if left to sit too long in the hot broth.

PREPARATION TIME: 25 minutes, plus 8 hours soaking the beans, making the stock and sauce (optional)
COOKING TIME: 3¼ hours on HIGH   **SERVES 4**

200g/7oz/1 cup dried cannellini beans, soaked in cold water for at least 8 hours

150g/5½oz courgettes, diced

150g/5½oz thin green beans, finely chopped

4 large garlic cloves, finely chopped

1 onion, finely chopped

1 celery stick, finely chopped

1 carrot, diced

1 leek, halved lengthways, thinly sliced and rinsed

800ml/28fl oz/scant 3½ cups Vegetable Stock (see page 169), ready-made stock or water, boiling, plus extra if needed

150ml/5fl oz/scant ⅔ cup passata

1 tbsp extra virgin olive oil, plus extra to serve

2 bay leaves, tied together with several rosemary and thyme sprigs

½ tsp caster sugar

4 large tomatoes

55g/2oz dried angel hair pasta, broken up

salt and freshly ground black pepper

freshly grated Parmesan cheese, to serve

1 recipe quantity Pesto Sauce (see page 171) or 4 tbsp ready-made fresh pesto, to serve

Bring a large, covered saucepan of unsalted water to the boil. Drain the beans and add them to the pan. Return to the boil and boil vigorously for 10 minutes. Drain and rinse the beans, then transfer them to the slow cooker.

Add all of the remaining ingredients, except the tomatoes and pasta, and season with pepper. Add extra stock to cover the beans, if necessary.

Cover the cooker with the lid and cook on HIGH for 3 hours until the beans are tender.

Meanwhile, use a sharp knife to cut a cross in the bottom of each tomato, then put them in a heatproof bowl and cover with boiling water. Leave to stand for 2–3 minutes, then drain. Peel off and discard the skins, then deseed and dice.

When the beans are tender, stir in the tomatoes and pasta and season with salt. Re-cover the cooker and cook for a further 15 minutes until the pasta is tender. Remove and discard the herb bundle and add a little more salt and pepper, if you like. Sprinkle with Parmesan, add a splash of olive oil and serve with a dollop of Pesto Sauce.

RUSTIC ITALIAN BEAN SOUP

The oil-rich Garlic Croûtons (see page 170) add texture and flavour to this simple soup. If you don't have time to make any, serve the soup with slices of toasted ciabatta bread instead.

PREPARATION TIME: 25 minutes, plus 8 hours soaking the beans, making the stock and croûtons (optional)
COOKING TIME: 2½ hours on HIGH   **SERVES 4**

200g/7oz/1 cup dried cannellini beans, soaked in cold water for at least 8 hours

1 carrot, diced

2 celery sticks, finely chopped

4 garlic cloves, finely chopped

1 onion, halved, and each half studded with 2 cloves

1 tbsp dried sage

1.25l/44fl oz/5 cups Vegetable Stock (see page 169), ready-made stock or water, boiling, plus extra if needed

1 tbsp extra virgin olive oil, plus extra to serve

2 tbsp finely chopped parsley leaves

salt and freshly ground black pepper

1 recipe quantity Garlic Croûtons (see page 170), to serve (optional)

Bring a large, covered saucepan of unsalted water to the boil. Drain the beans and add them to the pan. Return to the boil and boil vigorously for 10 minutes.

Meanwhile, put the carrot, celery, garlic, onion and sage in the slow cooker.

Drain and rinse the beans, then transfer them to the cooker. Pour over the stock and oil and season with pepper. Add extra stock to just cover the beans, if necessary.

Cover the cooker with the lid and cook on HIGH for 2½ hours until the beans are very tender. Remove and discard the onion and any loose cloves.

Strain the soup into a large bowl, reserving the cooking liquid. Purée half of the beans with a little of the reserved liquid in a blender or food processor until smooth. Return the mixture and the remaining beans to the cooker and slowly stir in the remaining reserved cooking liquid until the desired consistency is achieved. Season with salt and a little more pepper, if you like, and stir in the parsley. Sprinkle with Garlic Croûtons, if you like, drizzle with olive oil and serve.

APPLE SAUCE

PREPARATION TIME: 15 minutes
COOKING TIME: 8 hours on LOW
MAKES ABOUT 1kg/2lb 4oz

1.4kg/3lb 2oz tart apples, peeled, quartered and cored
1 cinnamon stick (optional)
4 tbsp caster sugar, plus extra to taste
finely grated zest of 1 lemon, plus extra to taste

Put the apples and cinnamon stick, if using, in the slow cooker and pour over 1l/35fl oz/4 cups water. The apples will not be completely covered.

Cover the cooker with the lid and cook on LOW for 8 hours until the apples are very tender. Remove and discard the cinnamon stick, if necessary.

Strain the sauce, reserving the cooking liquid (see Cook's Tip, below). Return the apples to the cooker and, using a potato masher or wooden spoon, mash to a texture as chunky as you like. Alternatively, process the sauce through a mouli-legume until smooth, then return to the cooker.

Stir in the sugar and lemon zest, adding a little more sugar and zest, if you like, and stir until the sugar dissolves. Serve hot or chilled.

If not serving immediately, leave the sauce to cool completely, then cover and chill. Keep refrigerated for up to 2 days, or freeze for up to 1 month.

COOK'S TIP
This recipe is a great way to take advantage of windfall apples – abundant and inexpensive in the autumn. Don't waste the flavoursome cooking liquid. Leave it to cool and you'll have a delicious apple juice. Try it chilled over ice with a little root ginger grated in.

BARBECUE SAUCE

PREPARATION TIME: 15 minutes, plus cooling and 24 hours chilling
COOKING TIME: 8 hours on LOW
MAKES ABOUT 875ml/30fl oz/3½ cups

2 tbsp sunflower oil
2 celery sticks, finely chopped
2 onions, finely chopped
4 large garlic cloves, crushed
375ml/13fl oz/1½ cups cider vinegar
165g/5¾oz/⅔ cup tomato purée
225g/8oz/1 cup firmly packed soft light brown sugar
4 tbsp molasses
4 tbsp Worcestershire sauce
2 tbsp Dijon mustard
4 tsp hot, smoked or sweet paprika
2 tsp celery seeds
½ tsp cayenne pepper
salt and freshly ground black pepper

Heat the oil in a saucepan over a high heat. Reduce the heat to medium, add the celery and onions and fry, stirring, for 2 minutes. Add the garlic and fry for a further 1–3 minutes until the onions are softened.

Add all of the remaining ingredients and stir until the sugar and molasses dissolve. Season with salt and pepper, then bring to the boil, stirring. Pour the sauce into the slow cooker, scraping the side of the pan with a rubber spatula.

Cover the cooker with the lid and cook on LOW for 8 hours. Pour the sauce into a blender or food processor and blend until smooth. Add a little more salt and pepper, if you like. Leave the sauce to cool completely, then cover and chill for 1 day to let the flavours blend. Serve hot or chilled. Keep any remaining sauce refrigerated for up to 2 weeks, or freeze for up to 1 month.

BOLOGNESE SAUCE

PREPARATION TIME: 30 minutes
COOKING TIME: 6 hours on LOW
MAKES ABOUT 900g/2lb

2 tbsp olive oil
30g/1oz smoked pancetta, chopped, or lardons
1 carrot, finely diced
1 celery stick, peeled and finely diced
1 onion, finely chopped
4 large garlic cloves, finely chopped
500g/1lb 2oz lean minced beef
4 tbsp Italian dried mixed herbs
2 tbsp plain white flour
250ml/9fl oz/1 cup dry red wine
800g/1lb 12oz/scant 3 cups tinned chopped tomatoes
4 tbsp passata
1½ tsp caster sugar
salt and freshly ground black pepper

Heat the oil in a frying pan over a high heat. Reduce the heat to low, add the pancetta and fry, stirring, for 1–2 minutes until it starts to crisp. Use a slotted spoon to transfer the pancetta to the slow cooker.

Pour off any excess fat from the pan, leaving about 2 tablespoons. Add the carrot, celery, onion and garlic and fry, stirring, for 8–10 minutes. Increase the heat to medium. Add the beef and herbs and fry for 2–3 minutes until browned. Stir in the flour and cook for 2 minutes. Add the wine, increase the heat to high and leave to boil until almost evaporated.

Transfer the meat mixture to the cooker and stir in the chopped tomatoes, passata and sugar, and season lightly with salt and pepper. Cover the cooker and cook on LOW for 6 hours, then serve.

If not serving immediately, leave the sauce to cool completely, then cover and chill. Keep refrigerated for up to 3 days, or freeze for up to 1 month.

EASY TOMATO SAUCE

PREPARATION TIME: 15 minutes
COOKING TIME: 4 hours on LOW
MAKES ABOUT 700ml/24fl oz/
  scant 3 cups

5 tbsp olive oil
2 onions, finely chopped
8 large garlic cloves, peeled
3 tbsp Italian dried mixed herbs
1.6kg/3lb 8oz tinned plum tomatoes
250ml/9fl oz/1 cup passata
1½ tsp caster sugar
salt and freshly ground black pepper

Heat 4 tablespoons of the oil in a large frying pan over a high heat. Reduce the heat to medium, add the onions and fry, stirring, for 5–8 minutes until just starting to turn golden. Add the garlic and fry for a further 1 minute.

Transfer the onions and garlic to the slow cooker and stir in the mixed herbs. Add the plum tomatoes, passata, sugar and the remaining oil and season with salt and pepper.

Cover the cooker with the lid and cook on LOW for 4 hours until the tomatoes have broken down and the sauce is thick.

Smash the garlic into the side of the container or remove it, depending on how garlicky you like your sauce, and serve. Alternatively, transfer to a blender or food processor and purée until smooth before serving.

If not serving immediately, leave the sauce to cool completely, then cover and chill. Keep refrigerated for up to 3 days, or freeze for up to 1 month.

MEAT & POULTRY

This is the chapter where the slow cooker really comes into its own, and, consequently, I have devoted more than half the book to the subject. The recipes here are drawn from cuisines around the world, and the flavours range from hot and spicy curries through fruity tagines to mild-tasting turkey simmered in apple juice.

I've included recipes you can leave to cook all day, ready for the evening, as well as a selection of quicker ones, such as the rice-based dishes. I've also developed recipes that are a complete meal-in-a-pot, such as Massaman Beef & Potato Curry (see page 97), so when you lift the lid off your cooker there isn't anything to do but serve and enjoy.

If you want to add dumplings to any of your slow cooker stews, use the recipe for Classic Beef Stew with Cheese & Herb Dumplings (see page 81) as a template. It is specifically cooked on a high setting so the liquid is hot enough for the dumplings to cook through and not become stodgy. The recipe also contains more stock than is specified in other recipes so the dumplings have plently of liquid to cook in.

If you're sceptical about cooking a whole chicken in a slow cooker, try the French 'Roast' Lemon & Thyme Chicken (see page 48). The skin isn't as crisp as when roasted in the oven, but the lemon butter keeps the breasts wonderfully flavourful and moist.

This chapter will also introduce you to inexpensive cuts of meat. If you've never tried ox cheeks or oxtails, for example, I urge you to. They appear so unpromising but the slow cooker miraculously tranforms them into tender, succulent meat.

◄ GREEK SPICED BEEF & ONION STEW (SEE PAGE 82)

CHICKEN JALFREZI

When I make the curry paste, I often make double the quantity and freeze the leftovers, saving even more time when I'm next in the mood for a spicy meal.

PREPARATION TIME: 25 minutes, plus making the curry paste and raita
COOKING TIME: 2 hours on HIGH   **SERVES 4**

900g/2lb chicken thighs, skin removed

30g/1oz ghee or 2 tbsp vegetable oil, peanut oil or sunflower oil

2 green peppers, halved lengthways, deseeded and sliced

2 red peppers, halved lengthways, deseeded and sliced

1 green chilli, deseeded if you like, and sliced

1 onion, thinly sliced

1 recipe quantity Jalfrezi Curry Paste (see page 170)

400g/14oz/scant 1⅔ cups tinned chopped tomatoes

a pinch of garam masala

salt and freshly ground black pepper

coriander leaves, to serve

1 recipe quantity Cucumber & Mint Raita or Cucumber & Tomato Raita (see page 172), to serve

cooked pilau or basmati rice, to serve

warm naan breads, to serve

Put the chicken in the slow cooker. Melt the ghee in a large frying pan over a high heat. Reduce the heat to medium, add the peppers, chilli and onion and fry, stirring, for 6–8 minutes until the onion is softened and just starting to brown. Stir in the jalfrezi paste and fry for a further 1 minute.

Add the chopped tomatoes and season with salt and pepper. Bring to the boil, stirring, then pour the mixture into the cooker.

Cover the cooker with the lid. Cook on HIGH for 2 hours until the juices from the chicken run clear when the thickest part of the meat is pierced with the tip of a sharp knife or skewer.

Add a little more salt and pepper, if you like, and sprinkle over the garam masala. Sprinkle with coriander and serve with Cucumber and Mint Raita, rice and naan breads.

CAJUN CHICKEN LIVER RICE

PREPARATION TIME: 25 minutes, plus making the stock (optional) and at least 5 minutes standing
COOKING TIME: 1½ hours on HIGH   **SERVES 4**

2 tbsp sunflower oil, plus extra if needed

2 celery sticks, finely chopped

2 green peppers, halved lengthways, deseeded and finely chopped

1 onion, finely chopped

4 spring onions, finely chopped, plus extra to serve

2 garlic cloves, finely chopped

2 tsp dried thyme

¼ tsp cayenne pepper

500g/1lb 2oz fresh or defrosted, frozen chicken livers, trimmed and halved

750ml/26fl oz/3 cups Chicken Stock (see page 168) or ready-made stock

280g/10oz/1½ cups easy-cook white rice

salt and freshly ground black pepper

chopped parsley leaves, to serve

hot pepper sauce, to serve

Heat the oil in a large frying pan over a high heat. Reduce the heat to medium, add the celery, peppers and onion and fry, stirring, for 2 minutes. Add the spring onions, garlic, thyme and cayenne pepper and fry for a further 5–7 minutes until the onions are softened and starting to turn golden.

Add the chicken livers to the pan, adding extra oil if necessary, and fry until they are browned all over but still pink in the centre.

Add the stock and bring to the boil, then pour the mixture into the slow cooker. Stir in the rice and season with salt and pepper.

Cover the cooker with the lid and cook on HIGH for 1½ hours until the chicken livers are cooked through and the rice is tender. Remove the lid and add a little more salt and pepper, if you like.

Switch the cooker off. Put a clean kitchen towel over the rice, re-cover with the lid and leave to stand for at least 5 minutes. The rice mixture can be left covered with the kitchen towel for up to 30 minutes. Just before serving, fluff up the rice with a fork. Sprinkle with parsley and spring onions and serve with some hot pepper sauce.

CHICKEN KATZU CURRY

PREPARATION TIME: 20 minutes, plus making the stock (optional)
COOKING TIME: 2 hours on HIGH   **SERVES 4**

250g/9oz carrots, thinly sliced

250g/9oz new potatoes, peeled and chopped

4 boneless, skinless chicken breasts,
about 185g/6½oz each

2 tbsp sunflower oil

1 onion, finely chopped

2 large garlic cloves, chopped

1 tbsp korma curry powder

1 tbsp ground ginger

500ml/17fl oz/2 cups Vegetable Stock (see page 169)
or ready-made stock

2 tbsp tomato purée

2 tbsp mango chutney

2 tbsp cornflour

salt and freshly ground black pepper

cooked jasmine rice, to serve

2 tbsp sesame seeds, toasted (see page 170), to serve

Put the carrots and potatoes in the slow cooker. Season the chicken breasts with salt and pepper and add to the cooker.

Heat 1 tablespoon of the oil in a large frying pan over a high heat. Reduce the heat to medium, add the onion and fry, stirring, for 2 minutes. Add the garlic, curry powder and ginger and stir for a further 1–3 minutes until the onion is softened.

Add the stock, tomato purée and mango chutney, stirring to dissolve the chutney, then season lightly with salt and pepper. Bring to the boil, stirring, then pour the mixture into the cooker.

Cover the cooker with the lid and cook on HIGH for 1½ hours.

Put the cornflour and 2 tablespoons cold water in a small bowl and stir until smooth, then stir the paste into the cooking liquid. Re-cover the cooker and cook for a further 30 minutes until the juices from the chicken run clear when the thickest part of the meat is pierced with the tip of a sharp knife or skewer, the vegetables are tender and the cooking juices have thickened slightly. Remove the chicken from the cooker, wrap in foil and leave to rest for at least 5 minutes. Re-cover the cooker and leave the setting on HIGH to keep the curry warm.

Cut the chicken into bite-sized pieces, then return it to the cooker. Add a little more salt and pepper, if you like. Spoon the curry over the rice, sprinkle with toasted sesame seeds and serve.

ASIAN-STYLE POACHED CHICKEN & PAK CHOI

PREPARATION TIME: 20 minutes, plus making the stock (optional)
COOKING TIME: 4 hours 5 minutes on HIGH   **SERVES 4**

a few coriander sprigs, with crushed stalks, plus extra leaves to serve

2 onions, 1 halved and 1 sliced

1 oven-ready chicken, about 1.5kg/3lb 5oz, any fat in the cavity removed

600ml/21fl oz/scant 2½ cups Chicken Stock (see page 168) or ready-made stock, boiling, plus extra if needed

125ml/4fl oz/½ cup dark soy sauce or mushroom soy sauce, plus extra to taste

4 tbsp rice wine

4 garlic cloves, sliced

2.5cm/1in piece of galangal, sliced

1 dried red Thai chilli, deseeded if you like

2 spring onions, thinly sliced

2 pak choi, quartered

ground Szechuan pepper or freshly ground black pepper

cooked long-grain rice, to serve

Put an upturned heatproof saucer in the slow cooker. (Check that the chicken will be able to sit on top of the saucer with the cooker lid in place.) Preheat the covered cooker on HIGH.

Put the coriander and halved onion in the chicken's cavity and season with pepper. Secure the opening with wooden cocktail sticks. Put the chicken in the cooker, breast-side down, then pour over the stock, soy sauce and rice wine. Add extra stock to fill the container, if necessary, leaving a 2.5cm/1in gap at the top of the pot. The chicken will not be completely covered with liquid. Push the sliced onion, garlic, galangal and chilli into the liquid.

Cover the cooker with the lid. Cook on HIGH for 3¾ hours until the juices from the chicken run clear when the thickest part of the meat is pierced with the tip of a sharp knife or skewer. Remove the chicken from the cooker, wrap in foil and leave to rest for about 10 mintues. Meanwhile, put the spring onions and pak choi in the cooker, re-cover and cook for a further 20 minutes until the pak choi is tender. Remove the pak choi from the cooker, and wrap in the foil with the chicken.

Pour the cooking liquid into a saucepan and bring to the boil, then boil vigorously for at least 3 minutes until reduced. Add a little more soy sauce and pepper, if you like. Remove the skin from the chicken and carve. Strain the cooking liquid, discarding the solids. Sprinkle the chicken with coriander and serve with the cooking liquid, pak choi and rice.

CHICKEN TAGINE

PREPARATION TIME: 20 minutes, plus making the stock (optional)
COOKING TIME: 1½ hours on HIGH   **SERVES 4**

1 tbsp olive oil, plus extra if needed

900g/2lb chicken thighs, skin removed

85g/3oz/½ cup green olives stuffed with pimientos

400g/14oz tinned chickpeas, drained and rinsed

135g/4¾oz/¾ cup ready-to-eat dried apricots

2 bay leaves, torn

2 preserved lemons, sliced

1 onion, chopped

4 garlic cloves, chopped

2 tbsp ground coriander

2 tbsp ground cumin

1 tbsp ground ginger

½ tsp dried chilli flakes, or to taste

a large pinch of saffron threads

600ml/21fl oz/scant 2½ cups Chicken Stock (see page 168), Vegetable Stock (see page 169) or ready-made stock

4cm/1½in piece of root ginger, or to taste

salt and freshly ground black pepper

chopped coriander leaves, to serve

cooked couscous, to serve

Heat the oil in a large frying pan over a high heat. Reduce the heat to medium. Add the chicken thighs, skin-side down, and fry for 3–5 minutes until golden brown, working in batches to avoid overcrowding the pan and adding extra oil, if necessary. Use a slotted spoon to transfer the chicken thighs to the slow cooker as they brown. Add the olives, chickpeas, dried apricots, bay leaves and preserved lemons to the cooker.

Pour off any excess fat from the pan, leaving about 1 tablespoon. Add the onion and fry, stirring, for 2 minutes. Add the garlic and spices and fry for a further 1–3 minutes until the onion is softened.

Add the stock and bring to the boil, scraping the bottom of the pan, then pour the mixture into the cooker and season lightly with salt and pepper. The chicken will not be completely covered with liquid.

Cover the cooker with the lid. Cook on HIGH for 1½ hours until the juices from the chicken run clear when the thickest part of the meat is pierced with the tip of a sharp knife or skewer. Use a large metal spoon to skim any excess fat from the surface of the cooking liquid. Remove and discard the bay leaves, then finely grate the unpeeled ginger directly into the pot and add a little more salt and pepper, if you like. Sprinkle with coriander and serve with couscous.

CHICKEN WITH TURKISH WALNUT SAUCE

PREPARATION TIME: 20 minutes
COOKING TIME: 3¾ hours on HIGH   **SERVES 4**

2 onions, 1 halved and 1 thinly sliced

1 handful of coriander, with crushed stalks

1 oven-ready chicken, about 1.5kg/3lb 5oz, any fat in the cavity removed

2 bay leaves

1 carrot, thinly sliced

1 celery stick, thinly sliced

1 cinnamon stick

½ tsp salt

freshly ground black pepper

chopped dill sprigs, shredded coriander leaves or chopped parsley leaves, to serve

pomegranate seeds, to serve

salad, to serve

WALNUT SAUCE

100g/3½oz/1 cup walnut halves

55g/2oz day-old bread, crusts removed and torn into pieces

125ml/4fl oz/½ cup single cream

a pinch of sweet paprika, or to taste

Put an upturned heatproof saucer in the slow cooker. (Check that the chicken will be able to sit on top of the saucer with the cooker lid in place.) Preheat the covered cooker on HIGH.

Put the halved onion and coriander in the chicken's cavity and season with salt and pepper. Secure the opening with wooden cocktail sticks. Put the chicken in the cooker, breast-side down, then push in the sliced onion, bay leaves, carrot, celery and cinnamon stick. Pour over enough water to fill the container, leaving a 2.5cm/1in gap at the top of the pot. Stir in the salt and season with pepper. The chicken will not be completely covered with liquid.

Cover the cooker with the lid. Cook on HIGH for 3¾ hours until the juices from the chicken run clear when the thickest part of the meat is pierced.

Meanwhile, make the sauce. Heat a frying pan over a high heat. Add the walnuts and dry-fry for 2–3 minutes, shaking the pan occasionally to ensure they do not burn. Transfer 75g/2½oz/¾ cup of the walnuts to a mini food processor. Add the bread and blitz until finely ground. Chop the remaining walnuts and leave to one side.

Remove the chicken from the cooker, wrap in foil and leave to rest for 10 minutes. Meanwhile, add the cream, paprika and 2 tablespoons of the cooking liquid to the mini food processor and process, adding more liquid to form a thick pouring sauce. Season with salt and pepper. Remove the skin from the chicken and carve. Spoon the sauce over the chicken, sprinkle with the chopped walnuts, dill and pomegranate seeds and serve with salad.

FRENCH 'ROAST' LEMON & THYME CHICKEN

PREPARATION TIME: 25 minutes, plus making the stock (optional)
COOKING TIME: 3¾ hours on HIGH   **SERVES 4**

30g/1oz butter, softened

8 thyme sprigs

finely grated zest of ½ lemon, with the whole lemon reserved and pricked all over with a fork

1 oven-ready chicken, about 1.5kg/3lb 5oz, any fat in the cavity removed

2 garlic cloves, smashed

1 shallot, sliced

30g/1oz goose fat or duck fat, or 2 tbsp olive oil

1 celery stick, chopped

1 onion, sliced

250ml/9fl oz/1 cup Chicken Stock (see page 168) or ready-made stock

125ml/4fl oz/½ cup dry white wine

salt and freshly ground black pepper

sautéed potatoes, to serve

Put an upturned heatproof saucer in the slow cooker. (Check that the chicken will be able to sit on top of the saucer with the cooker lid in place.) Preheat the covered cooker on HIGH.

Mix together the butter, leaves from 3 of the thyme sprigs and the lemon zest and season with salt and pepper. Carefully ease your hand under the skin of the chicken, then gently lift the skin, taking care not to tear it. Ease three-quarters of the butter under the skin and rub it over the flesh, then rub the remaining butter over the skin.

Put the remaining thyme in the chicken's cavity with the garlic, shallot and whole lemon and season. Secure the opening with wooden cocktail sticks. Season the breasts with salt and pepper.

Melt the goose fat in a frying pan over a medium-high heat. Add the chicken and fry, breast-side down, for 3 minutes until golden. Put the celery and onion in the cooker, add the chicken and cover with the lid.

Pour off any excess fat from the pan. Add the stock and wine and boil, scraping the bottom, until reduced by about one-third, then pour into the cooker. The chicken will not be completely covered with liquid. Re-cover the cooker and cook on HIGH for 3¾ hours until the juices run clear when the thickest part of the meat is pierced.

Remove the chicken, wrap in foil and leave to rest for 5 minutes. Meanwhile, skim any excess fat from the cooking liquid. Strain the cooking liquid and the juices from the chicken cavity into a saucepan. Boil until reduced by one-third. Spoon the juices over the chicken and serve with sautéed potatoes.

CHICKEN & SMOKED HAM GUMBO

PREPARATION TIME: 35 minutes, plus making the stock (optional)
COOKING TIME: 1½ hours on HIGH   **SERVES 4**

3 tbsp corn oil

60g/2¼oz/½ cup plain white flour

1 large onion, chopped

4 garlic cloves, chopped

1 celery stick, halved lengthways and chopped

1 green pepper, halved lengthways, deseeded and diced

350ml/12fl oz/scant 1½ cups Chicken Stock (see page 168), Vegetable Stock (see page 169) or ready-made stock

400g/14oz/scant 1⅔ cups tinned chopped tomatoes

4 okra, trimmed and sliced

1 tbsp dried thyme

1 tsp smoked paprika

¼ tsp dried chilli flakes, or to taste

150g/5½oz/¾ cup fresh or defrosted, frozen sweetcorn kernels

2 tbsp tomato purée

a pinch of light brown sugar

400g/14oz boneless, skinless chicken thighs, cut into thick strips

280g/10oz smoked ham, trimmed and diced

2 bay leaves

4 tbsp chopped parsley leaves, plus extra to serve

1 tsp lemon juice, to taste (optional)

salt and freshly ground black pepper

cooked American long-grain rice, to serve

hot pepper sauce, to serve

Heat the oil in a large frying pan over a high heat. Reduce the heat to medium-low, then sprinkle over the flour and stir to make a thick paste. Continue stirring for 15–20 minutes until the paste turns a hazelnut colour. It will be very slow to change colour, then change quickly, so watch closely so that it does not burn.

Add the onion, garlic, celery and pepper and stir for a further 3–5 minutes until the onion is softened.

Add the stock, chopped tomatoes, okra, thyme, paprika, chilli flakes, sweetcorn, tomato purée and brown sugar and bring to the boil, stirring, then pour the mixture into the slow cooker. Stir in the chicken, ham and bay leaves and season with salt and pepper.

Cover the cooker with the lid. Cook on HIGH for 1½ hours until the juices from the chicken run clear when the thickest part of the meat is pierced with the tip of a sharp knife or skewer. Remove and discard the bay leaves. Stir in the parsley and lemon juice, if using, and add a little more salt and pepper, if you like. Spoon the gumbo over the rice, sprinkle with parsley and serve with some hot pepper sauce.

COOK'S TIP
If you need to defrost frozen corn kernels in a hurry, put them in a sieve and rinse under hot running water. Alternatively, soak the kernels in a bowl of boiling water for 3 minutes, then drain well.

GLAZED DRUMSTICKS

PREPARATION TIME: 10 minutes, plus
up to 24 hours marinating
COOKING TIME: 2 hours on HIGH   **SERVES 4**

150ml/5fl oz/scant ⅔ cup light soy sauce
2 tbsp rice wine vinegar
5 tbsp dark brown sugar
4 large garlic cloves, smashed
1 tbsp ground coriander
1 tbsp ground cumin
4 spring onions, finely chopped, plus extra to serve
1 handful of coriander leaves, finely chopped
8 chicken drumsticks, skin removed
2 tbsp arrowroot or cornflour
200g/7oz mangetout, trimmed
freshly ground black pepper
cooked rice or noodles, to serve

Put the soy sauce, vinegar, brown sugar, garlic,
ground coriander, cumin, spring onions and
coriander in a large non-metallic bowl and stir until
the sugar dissolves. Add the drumsticks, then rub
the mixture all over them. Season with pepper.
Cover and marinate in the fridge for up to 24 hours.

Transfer the drumsticks and all of the marinade
to the slow cooker. The drumsticks will not be
completely covered with liquid.

Cover the cooker with the lid and cook on HIGH
for 1½ hours, turning once after 1 hour. Put the
arrowroot and 2 tablespoons cold water in a bowl
and stir until smooth, then stir the paste into the
cooking liquid. Re-cover the cooker and cook for
15 minutes. Add the mangetout, re-cover and cook
for 15 minutes until the juices from the chicken run
clear when the thickest part of the meat is pierced.
Sprinkle with spring onions and serve with rice.

TURKEY & RED CABBAGE

PREPARATION TIME: 10 minutes
COOKING TIME: 4 hours on HIGH   **SERVES 4**

1 tbsp smoked or sweet paprika, or to taste
700g/1lb 9oz boneless, skinless turkey breast
400g/14oz tinned cannellini beans, drained and rinsed
2 bay leaves, torn
1 tbsp dried tarragon or parsley
turkey bones (optional)
500ml/17fl oz/2 cups apple juice, plus extra if needed
200g/7oz red cabbage, cored and thinly sliced
1 long strip of lemon rind, pith removed
salt and freshly ground black pepper
chopped parsley leaves, to serve

Rub the paprika all over the turkey breast, then put
it in the slow cooker. Add the beans to the cooker,
tucking them down around the turkey. Add the bay
leaves, tarragon and turkey bones, if using.

Pour over the apple juice, making sure the beans
are covered. The turkey breast might not be
covered with liquid. Season with salt and pepper.

Cover the cooker with the lid. Cook on HIGH for
3½ hours until the juices from the turkey run clear
when the thickest part of the meat is pierced with
the tip of a sharp knife or skewer. Remove the
turkey from the cooker, wrap in foil and leave to
rest for about 10 minutes.

Meanwhile, skim any excess fat from the cooking
liquid. Add the cabbage and lemon rind. Re-cover
the cooker and cook for 30 minutes until the
cabbage is tender. Remove and discard the bay
leaves and lemon rind, then slice the turkey. Spoon
the cooking liquid over the turkey, cabbage and
beans, sprinkle with parsley and serve.

TURKEY, SWEET POTATO & SWEETCORN CHILLI

This is a great one-pot dinner for when you want a simple meal. Its depth of flavour comes from the ancho chilli powder, but if you can't find any, use 2 tablespoons of chilli con carne seasoning and omit the ground cumin from the ingredients.

PREPARATION TIME: 15 minutes, plus making the tortilla chips (optional)
COOKING TIME: 2¼ hours on HIGH   **SERVES 4**

4 tbsp tomato purée

2 tbsp sunflower oil

1 onion, finely chopped

2 large garlic cloves, crushed

1 tbsp ancho chilli powder, or to taste

1½ tsp ground cumin

a pinch of cayenne pepper (optional)

500g/1lb 2oz lean minced turkey

400g/14oz/scant 1⅔ cups tinned chopped tomatoes

200g/7oz orange-fleshed sweet potato, finely diced

200g/7oz tinned pinto beans, drained and rinsed

200g/7oz tinned sweetcorn kernels, drained and rinsed

1 bay leaf

salt and freshly ground black pepper

cooked white rice, to serve

chopped coriander or parsley leaves, to serve

1 recipe quantity Tortilla Chips (see page 174) or corn chips, to serve (optional)

Put the tomato purée and 4 tablespoons water in a small bowl and stir until dissolved, then leave to one side.

Heat 1 tablespoon of the oil in a large frying pan over a high heat. Reduce the heat to medium, add the onion and fry, stirring, for 2 minutes. Add the garlic, chilli powder, cumin and cayenne pepper, if using, and stir for a further 1–3 minutes until the onion is softened. Use a slotted spoon to transfer the mixture to the slow cooker.

Heat the remaining oil in the pan. Add the turkey and fry for 2–3 minutes, breaking up the meat, until browned all over. Use a slotted spoon to transfer the turkey to the cooker, leaving behind as much oil as possible. Add the tomato purée mixture and all of the remaining ingredients to the cooker and stir. Season with salt and pepper.

Cover the cooker with the lid. Cook on HIGH for 2¼ hours, stirring once halfway through, until the turkey is tender and the flavours are blended. Remove and discard the bay leaf and add a little more salt and pepper, if you like. Spoon the chilli over the rice, sprinkle with coriander and serve with Tortilla Chips, if you like.

DUCK TAGINE

PREPARATION TIME: 20 minutes
COOKING TIME: 1½ hours on HIGH   **SERVES 4**

4 duck legs, about 250g/9oz each, skin scored

100g/3½oz cooking chorizo, skinned and sliced

1 courgette, halved lengthways and thinly sliced

1 tbsp olive oil, if needed

1 onion, thinly sliced

2 garlic cloves, finely chopped

1 tbsp fennel seeds

1 tbsp dried thyme

2 tsp ground coriander

a pinch of dried chilli flakes, or to taste

125ml/4fl oz/½ cup dry white wine

400g/14oz/scant 1⅔ cups tinned chopped tomatoes

2 long strips of orange rind, pith removed

12 pitted prunes

2 tbsp freshly squeezed orange juice, or to taste (optional)

salt and freshly ground black pepper

chopped coriander leaves, to serve

pine nuts, toasted (see page 170), to serve

cooked couscous, to serve

Heat a heavy-based frying pan over a high heat. Add the duck legs, skin-side down, and fry for 3–5 minutes until the fat under the skin has melted into the pan. Use a slotted spoon to transfer the duck legs to the slow cooker as they brown.

Pour off any excess fat from the pan, leaving about 1 tablespoon. Reduce the heat to medium, add the chorizo and fry, stirring, for 1–2 minutes until it gives off its fat and starts to crisp. Use a slotted spoon to transfer the chorizo to the cooker, then add the courgette to the cooker.

If there is less than 1 tablespoon of fat remaining in the pan, add the oil and heat. When the oil is hot, add the onion and fry, stirring, for 2 minutes. Add the garlic, fennel seeds, thyme, ground coriander and chilli flakes and fry for a further 1–3 minutes until the onion is softened. Pour over the wine, bring to the boil and boil until almost evaporated. Add the chopped tomatoes and orange rind and season with salt and pepper. Bring to the boil, scraping the bottom of the pan, then pour the mixture into the cooker. The ingredients in the cooker will not be completely covered with liquid. Add the prunes, tucking them down among the duck legs.

Cover the cooker with the lid. Cook on HIGH for 1½ hours until the juices from the duck run clear when the thickest part of the meat is pierced with the tip of a sharp knife or skewer. Remove and discard the orange rind. Season with a little more salt and pepper, if you like, and stir in the orange juice, if using. Sprinkle with coriander and toasted pine nuts and serve with couscous.

VIETNAMESE CARAMEL PORK & CARROTS

Heating sugar and water to make caramel isn't difficult but it does take practice to heat the syrup until it is dark enough to have a rich, deep flavour without burning it. To gauge the colour accurately, use a stainless-steel pan, rather than a dark one. Take care when you stop the caramel cooking, because the sauce will splutter.

PREPARATION TIME: 20 minutes, plus pickling the bean sprouts (optional)
COOKING TIME: 8¼ hours on LOW   **SERVES 4**

280g/10oz carrots, thinly sliced

2 red Thai shallots or 1 French shallot, halved lengthways and sliced

1 lemongrass stalk, outer layer removed, bruised and cut in half

750g/1lb 10oz boneless pork leg, trimmed of fat and cut into large chunks

chopped salted peanuts, to serve

coriander leaves, to serve

cooked jasmine rice, to serve

1 recipe quantity Pickled Bean Sprouts (see page 173), to serve (optional)

VIETNAMESE CARAMEL SAUCE

150g/5½oz/heaped ¾ cup soft light brown sugar

1 tbsp fish sauce, plus extra to taste

1½ tsp lime juice, plus extra to taste

To make the caramel sauce, put the sugar and 2 tablespoons water in a saucepan over a medium heat and stir until the sugar dissolves. Increase the heat to high and boil, without stirring, until the caramel turns a dark golden brown colour. Watch closely because it can burn quickly. Immediately remove the pan from the heat and add the fish sauce and lime juice to stop the cooking process.

Put the carrots, shallots and lemongrass in the slow cooker. Add the pork and pour over the caramel sauce.

Cover the cooker with the lid and cook on LOW for 4 hours, then stir through to prevent the pork and carrots from sticking together. Re-cover the cooker as quickly as possible and cook for a further 4¼ hours until the pork is tender. Remove the pork and carrots from the cooker, wrap in foil and keep warm.

Strain the cooking liquid into a small saucepan, discarding the solids, and bring to the boil over a high heat. Boil for 3 minutes until the cooking liquid has reduced to about 125ml/4fl oz/½ cup. Add a little more fish sauce and lime juice, if you like. Stir in the pork and carrots and toss well to coat. Sprinkle with peanuts and coriander and serve with rice and Pickled Bean Sprouts, if you like.

SOUTHERN 'BAKED' BEANS WITH SMOKED HAM

PREPARATION TIME: 20 minutes, plus making the stock (optional)
COOKING TIME: 1 hour on HIGH, plus 8 hours on LOW   **SERVES 4**

1 bone-in smoked gammon hock, about 1.4kg/3lb 2oz

4 tbsp Vegetable Stock (see page 169), ready-made stock or water

400g/14oz/scant 1⅔ cups tinned chopped tomatoes

125g/4½oz/⅔ cup soft light brown sugar

2 bay leaves, torn

2 large garlic cloves, finely chopped

1 onion, finely chopped

1 tbsp dried thyme

2 tsp ground cumin

½ tsp dried chilli flakes, or to taste

800g/1lb 12oz tinned borlotti beans or pinto beans, drained and rinsed

salt and freshly ground black pepper

chopped parsley leaves, to serve

cornbread or cooked American long-grain rice, to serve (optional)

Put the gammon hock in a large saucepan and cover with water. Cover with a lid and bring to the boil over a high heat.

Meanwhile, put the stock, chopped tomatoes, brown sugar, bay leaves, garlic, onion, thyme, cumin and chilli flakes in the slow cooker, stirring to dissolve the sugar. Season with salt and pepper, remembering the gammon might still be salty.

When the gammon water boils, transfer the hock to a large colander and rinse well. Transfer the gammon to the slow cooker.

Add the beans to the cooker, tucking them down around the hock. The gammon and all the beans may not be completely covered with liquid.

Cover the cooker with the lid and cook on HIGH for 1 hour, then switch the cooker to LOW and cook for a further 8 hours until the gammon is tender and the meat is falling off the bone. Remove the gammon from the cooker and leave to cool slightly. Remove and discard the bay leaves. Re-cover the cooker to keep the beans warm.

When the gammon is cool enough to handle, remove all the meat from the bone, discarding the fat, gristle and skin. Cut the meat into portions, then return to the cooker to heat through, if necessary. Season with salt and a little more pepper, if you like. Sprinkle with parsley and serve with cornbread, if you like.

COWBOY PORK & BEANS

PREPARATION TIME: 25 minutes, plus making the stock (optional)
COOKING TIME: 5 hours on HIGH   **SERVES 4**

1 tbsp sunflower oil

700g/1lb 9oz belly of pork, cut into strips along the grain, then cut into bite-sized pieces

400g/14oz tinned red kidney beans, drained and rinsed

400g/14oz tinned black beans, drained and rinsed

1 onion, finely chopped

2 garlic cloves, finely chopped

1 tbsp ground coriander

1 tbsp ground cumin

1 tbsp dried thyme or dried oregano

½ tsp cayenne pepper, or to taste

400g/14oz/scant 1⅔ cups tinned chopped tomatoes

250ml/9fl oz/1 cup Vegetable Stock (see page 169), Beef Stock (see page 168) or ready-made stock, plus extra if needed

280g/10oz carrots, thinly sliced

2 tbsp tomato purée

2 tbsp molasses or dark brown sugar

1 tsp Worcestershire sauce, or to taste

salt and freshly ground black pepper

chopped parsley leaves, to serve

cooked American long-grain rice, to serve

Heat the oil in a large frying pan over a high heat. Add the pork and fry for 3–5 minutes until browned on all sides and as much fat as possible has melted into the pan, working in batches, if necessary. Watch closely, making sure that the edges do not burn. Transfer the pork to the slow cooker, then add all the beans.

Pour off any excess fat from the pan, leaving about 1 tablespoon. Add the onion and fry, stirring, for 2 minutes. Add the garlic, coriander, cumin, thyme and cayenne pepper and fry for a further 1–3 minutes until the onion is softened.

Add the chopped tomatoes, stock, carrots, tomato purée and molasses and season with salt and pepper. Bring to the boil, stirring, then pour the mixture into the cooker. There should be enough liquid to cover the pork and beans, but do not worry if they are not completely submerged.

Cover the cooker with the lid and cook on HIGH for 5 hours until the pork is tender. Stir in the Worcestershire sauce and add a little more pepper, if you like. Sprinkle with parsley and serve with rice.

ITALIAN PORK STEW WITH SUMMER HERBS

Don't be alarmed by the quantity of dried herbs in this recipe – it isn't a typing error! After the stew simmers for eight hours, the herbs mellow and the flavour of mint shines through. I find this dish particularly welcome in the middle of winter, when dried herbs really come into their own.

PREPARATION TIME: 25 minutes, plus making the stock (optional)
COOKING TIME: 8 hours on LOW   **SERVES 4**

750g/1lb 10oz boneless pork shoulder, trimmed of fat and cut into large chunks

400g/14oz tinned chickpeas, drained and rinsed

400g/14oz tinned plum tomatoes

2 tbsp olive oil

1 onion, finely chopped

1 carrot, finely chopped

1 celery stick, finely chopped

4 garlic cloves, finely chopped

250ml/9fl oz/1 cup passata

125ml/4fl oz/½ cup Vegetable Stock (see page 169) or ready-made stock, plus extra if needed

2–3 tbsp dried mint

1 tbsp dried thyme

1 tbsp dried oregano

a pinch of caster sugar

salt and freshly ground black pepper

finely shredded mint or chopped parsley leaves, to serve

soft polenta, to serve

Put the pork, chickpeas and plum tomatoes in the slow cooker.

Heat the oil in a large frying pan over a high heat. Reduce the heat to medium, add the onion, carrot and celery and fry, stirring, for 2 minutes. Add the garlic and fry for a further 1–3 minutes until the onion is softened.

Add the passata, stock, dried herbs and sugar, then season with salt and pepper and bring to the boil. Boil, stirring, for 3 minutes until the liquid has reduced by about one-third, then pour the mixture into the cooker. Stir well and add extra stock, if necessary, to just cover the chickpeas.

Cover the cooker with the lid and cook on LOW for 8 hours until the pork is tender. Add a little more salt and pepper, if you like. Sprinkle with mint and serve with soft polenta.

PORK PAPRIKASH

PREPARATION TIME: 30 minutes
COOKING TIME: 8 hours on LOW, plus 30 minutes on HIGH   **SERVES 4**

700g/1lb 9oz boneless pork shoulder, trimmed of fat and cut into large chunks

2 tbsp sunflower oil, plus extra if needed

1 large onion, finely chopped

600g/1lb 5oz chestnut mushrooms, sliced

1 tbsp smoked paprika

1 tbsp dried dill

1 tbsp cornflour

200ml/7fl oz/scant 1 cup condensed cream of mushroom soup

2 green peppers, halved lengthways, deseeded and diced

4 tbsp soured cream

280g/10oz dried tagliatelle or other flat noodles

30g/1oz butter

salt and freshly ground black pepper

chopped parsley leaves or chopped dill, to serve

Season the pork with salt and pepper. Heat the oil in a large frying pan over a high heat. Reduce the heat to medium, add the pork and fry for 3–5 minutes until browned on all sides, working in batches to avoid overcrowding the pan, and adding extra oil, if necessary. Use a slotted spoon to transfer the pork to the slow cooker.

Add the onion to the pan and fry, stirring, for 3–5 minutes until softened. Add the mushrooms, sprinkle with salt and fry for 5–8 minutes until all the liquid is absorbed, working in batches, if necessary. Sprinkle paprika and dill over the mushrooms and stir for 30 seconds.

Put the cornflour and 2 tablespoons cold water in a small bowl and stir until smooth. Add the cornflour paste and mushroom soup to the pan and bring to the boil, scraping the bottom of the pan. Pour the mixture into the cooker and stir well. Season lightly with salt and pepper.

Cover the cooker with the lid and cook on LOW for 8 hours. Stir in the peppers and soured cream. Switch the cooker to HIGH, re-cover and cook for 30 minutes until the pork and peppers are tender.

Twenty minutes before serving, bring a large saucepan of salted water to the boil. Add the tagliatelle and cook for 10 minutes, or according to the packet instructions, until tender. Drain well, shaking off any excess water, then return to the hot pan. Add the butter and stir until melted. Spoon the paprikash over the tagliatelle and season with a little more salt and pepper, if you like. Sprinkle with parsley and serve.

HAM WITH EGG & PARSLEY SAUCE

PREPARATION TIME: 20 minutes, plus making the stock (optional) and sauce
COOKING TIME: 9½ hours on LOW, plus 30 minutes on HIGH   **SERVES 4**

1 unsmoked gammon knuckle, about 1.4kg/3 lb 2oz

750ml/26fl oz/3 cups Vegetable Stock (see page 169) or ready-made stock, plus extra if needed

4 cloves

2 bay leaves, torn

280g/10oz white cabbage, cored and sliced

salt and freshly ground black pepper

1 recipe quantity Egg & Parsley Sauce (see page 172), to serve

boiled new potatoes, to serve

Put the gammon knuckle in a large saucepan and cover with water. Cover with a lid and bring to the boil over a high heat. When the gammon water boils, transfer the knuckle to a large colander and drain and rinse well. Transfer the gammon to the slow cooker. Add the stock, cloves and bay leaves, adding extra stock to cover the gammon, if necessary. Season with pepper.

Cover the cooker with the lid and cook on LOW for 9½ hours. Use a large metal spoon to skim any excess fat from the surface of the cooking liquid. Remove and discard the cloves and bay leaves. Season with salt and a little more pepper, if you like, remembering the gammon might have made the cooking liquid salty. Stir in the cabbage.

Switch the cooker to HIGH, re-cover and cook for 30 minutes until the gammon and cabbage are tender. Remove the knuckle from the cooker and leave to cool slightly. Re-cover the cooker to keep the cabbage warm.

When the gammon is cool enough to handle, remove all the meat from the bone, discarding the fat, gristle and skin. Cut the meat into portions, then remove the cabbage from the cooker, using a slotted spoon, and shake off any excess liquid. Serve the gammon and cabbage with Egg & Parsley Sauce and with new potatoes.

CHORIZO & BLACK BEAN RICE

I developed this version of the Spanish festival dish *Moros y Christianos*, for a quick and easy midweek dinner. The chorizo adds piquancy and extra protein. For a vegetarian version, omit the chorizo and fry the onion with the garlic, chilli and spices listed, then add 1 teaspoon of smoked paprika and cayenne pepper.

PREPARATION TIME: 20 minutes, plus making the stock (optional) and at least 5 minutes standing
COOKING TIME: 1½ hours on HIGH   **SERVES 4**

1 tbsp olive oil

80g/2¾oz cooking chorizo, skinned and diced

1 large onion, finely chopped

4 large garlic cloves, finely chopped

1 green chilli, deseeded if you like, and thinly sliced

1 tbsp dried dill

1 tsp ground cumin

750ml/26fl oz/3 cups Vegetable Stock (see page 169) or ready-made stock

400g/14oz tinned black beans, drained and rinsed

280g/10oz/1½ cups easy-cook white rice

2 sun-dried tomatoes in oil, drained and thinly sliced

2 tbsp finely chopped parsley leaves

salt and freshly ground black pepper

Heat the oil in a large frying pan over a high heat. Reduce the heat to medium, add the chorizo and fry, stirring, for 1–2 minutes until it gives off its fat and starts to crisp. Use a slotted spoon to transfer the chorizo to the slow cooker.

Pour off any excess fat from the pan, leaving about 1 tablespoon. Add the onion and fry, stirring, for 2 minutes. Add the garlic, chilli, dill and cumin and fry for a further 1–3 minutes until the onion is softened.

Add the stock and bring to the boil, stirring, then pour the mixture into the cooker. Stir in the beans, rice and sun-dried tomatoes and season with salt and pepper.

Cover the cooker with the lid and cook on HIGH for 1½ hours until the rice is tender. Stir in the parsley and add a little more salt and pepper, if you like.

Switch the cooker off. Put a clean kitchen towel over the rice, re-cover with the lid and leave to stand for at least 5 minutes. The rice can be left covered with the kitchen towel for up to 30 minutes. Just before serving, fluff up the rice with a fork. Serve hot.

✳

PULLED PORK

PREPARATION TIME: 10 minutes
COOKING TIME: 12 hours on LOW   SERVES 4

2 tbsp soft light brown sugar
1 tsp sweet paprika
2 tsp dried rosemary or thyme
½ tsp ground ginger
finely grated zest of 1 large lemon
1kg/2lb 4oz piece of boneless pork shoulder,
    with the skin and outer layer of fat removed
2 onions, sliced
185ml/6fl oz/¾ cup dry white wine
salt and freshly ground black pepper
mashed potatoes, to serve

Combine the brown sugar, paprika, rosemary, ginger and lemon zest in a bowl, then season with salt and pepper. Rub the mixture all over the pork. Put the pork, onions and wine in the slow cooker.

Cover the cooker with the lid and cook on LOW for 12 hours until the pork is very tender and falling apart. Gently remove the pork from the cooker, wrap tightly in foil and leave to rest for 10 minutes.

Meanwhile, skim any excess fat from the cooking liquid. Add a little more salt and pepper, if you like. Re-cover the cooker with the lid to keep the cooking liquid warm.

Unwrap the pork, transfer to a rimmed plate to catch any juices. Use two forks to pull apart and shred the meat. Pour any remaining juices into the cooking liquid. Spoon the cooking liquid over the pork and serve with mashed potatoes.

 ✳

PORK & SAUERKRAUT

PREPARATION TIME: 12 minutes,
    plus making the apple sauce (optional)
COOKING TIME: 2½ hours on HIGH   SERVES 4

500g/1lb 2oz/generous 3¾ cups sauerkraut, drained
200g/7oz/¾ cup Apple Sauce (see page 33) or ready-
    made apple sauce
1 large carrot, coarsely grated
2–4 tbsp soft brown sugar, to taste
2 tbsp orange juice
1 tsp smoked or sweet paprika, or to taste
4 boneless pork steaks, about 150g/5½oz each and
    2.5cm/1in thick
400g/14oz new potatoes, peeled and thinly sliced
salt and freshly ground black pepper
chopped parsley leaves, to serve

Mix together the sauerkraut, apple sauce, carrot, brown sugar, orange juice and paprika in a bowl. Season with salt and pepper and leave to one side. Season both sides of the pork steaks with salt and pepper.

Arrange the potatoes in a single layer, if possible, on the base of the slow cooker container. Add half of the sauerkraut mixture, then add the steaks in a single layer and top with the remaining sauerkraut mixture.

Cover the cooker with the lid and cook on HIGH for 2½ hours until the pork is tender when pierced with the tip of a sharp knife or skewer. Add a little more salt and pepper, if you like. Sprinkle with parsley and serve.

CHINESE BELLY OF PORK

This recipe produces a sweet-and-savoury cooking juice, ideal for serving with rice.

PREPARATION TIME: 20 minutes, plus 1 hour marinating
COOKING TIME: 5 hours on HIGH   **SERVES 4**

2 tbsp oyster sauce

2 tbsp dark soy sauce, or to taste

4 tsp sweet soy sauce, or to taste

2 tsp sweet chilli sauce

600g/1lb 5oz belly of pork, cut into strips along the grain, then cut into bite-sized pieces

2 tbsp garlic-infused sunflower oil

2 tbsp clear honey

2.5cm/1in piece of galangal, peeled and sliced

4 large garlic cloves, smashed

freshly ground black pepper

sesame oil, to serve

sesame seeds, toasted (see page 170), to serve

chopped coriander leaves, to serve

cooked short-grain white rice, to serve

Mix together 1 tablespoon of the oyster sauce, 1 tablespoon of the dark soy sauce, 2 teaspoons of the sweet soy sauce and 1 teaspoon of the chilli sauce in a bowl. Add the pork, then use your hands to rub the marinade all over the meat. Cover and leave to marinate for 1 hour at room temperature.

Remove the pork from the marinade and reserve the marinade. Pat the pork dry with kitchen paper. Heat the oil in a large frying pan over a high heat. Add the pork and fry for 3–5 minutes until browned on all sides and as much fat as possible has melted into the pan, working in batches, if necessary. Watch closely so the edges do not burn. Transfer the pork to the slow cooker.

Discard the fat in the pan, then wipe the bottom of the pan with kitchen paper. Add the remaining oyster sauce, dark soy sauce, sweet soy sauce and chilli sauce, honey, galangal, garlic, reserved marinade and 125ml/4fl oz/½ cup water and bring to the boil, stirring to dissolve the honey. Season with pepper, then pour over the pork.

Cover the cooker with the lid and cook on HIGH for 5 hours until the pork is tender. Add a little more pepper or soy sauce, if you like. Transfer the pork to a bowl, using a slotted spoon. Skim any excess fat from the cooking liquid, then remove and discard the galangal and garlic. Spoon the cooking liquid over the pork. Drizzle with sesame oil, sprinkle with toasted sesame seeds and coriander and serve with rice.

SAUSAGE HOTPOT

This is a regular busy-day meal in my house. Not only is it fantastically easy, the variations are endless. You can use whatever tinned pulses you have, and it's a great way to use up just about any vegetable – I particularly like to add chopped butternut squash. Spicy Italian sausages work really well, too. And, if I'm in a real hurry, I just skip frying the sausages, onions and peppers.

PREPARATION TIME: 20 minutes, plus making the stock (optional)
COOKING TIME: 4 hours on LOW   **SERVES 4**

1 tbsp olive oil

8 good-quality sausages, such as Cumberland or pork and fennel, pricked with a fork

1 large onion, finely chopped

2 large garlic cloves, crushed

1 green pepper, halved lengthways, deseeded and thickly sliced

1 red pepper, halved lengthways, deseeded and thickly sliced

400g/14oz tinned pulses, such as borlotti beans, butter beans, cannellini beans, chickpeas or kidney beans, drained and rinsed

400g/14oz/scant 1⅔ cups tinned chopped tomatoes with herbs

60ml/2fl oz/¼ cup Beef Stock (see page 168), Vegetable Stock (see page 169) or ready-made stock

2 bay leaves

Worcestershire sauce

freshly ground black pepper

chopped parsley leaves, to serve

Dijon, wholegrain or German sweet mustard, to serve

Heat a large frying pan over a high heat. Reduce the heat to medium, add the oil and sausages and fry for 3–5 minutes until browned all over, working in batches to avoid overcrowding the pan, if necessary. Use a slotted spoon to transfer the sausages to the slow cooker as they brown.

Pour off any excess oil from the pan, leaving about 1 tablespoon. Add the onion and fry, stirring, for 2 minutes. Add the garlic and peppers and fry for a further 1–3 minutes until the onion is softened. Use a slotted spoon to transfer the vegetables to the cooker.

Stir in the pulses, chopped tomatoes, stock and bay leaves and season with Worcestershire sauce and pepper. The ingredients will not be completely covered with liquid.

Cover the cooker with the lid. Cook on LOW for 4 hours until the sausages are cooked through and the peppers are tender. Remove and discard the bay leaves and add a little more Worcestershire sauce and pepper, if you like. Sprinkle with parsley and serve with some mustard.

ROGAN JOSH

PREPARATION TIME: 30 minutes, plus making the raita (optional)
COOKING TIME: 6 hours on LOW   **SERVES 4**

2 garlic cloves, coarsely chopped

4cm/1½in piece of root ginger, peeled and coarsely chopped

40g/1½oz ghee or 3 tbsp groundnut oil or sunflower oil, plus extra if needed

750g/1lb 10oz boneless lamb shoulder, trimmed of fat and cut into large chunks

2 onions, finely chopped

5 green cardamom pods, lightly crushed

4 cloves

2 cinnamon sticks

2 tsp ground cumin

1 tsp ground coriander

1 tsp sweet paprika

½ tsp Kashmiri chilli powder or cayenne pepper, or to taste

4 tbsp tomato purée

2 bay leaves

125g/4½oz/½ cup natural yogurt

½ tsp garam masala

salt and freshly ground black pepper

coriander leaves, to serve

cooked basmati rice, to serve

1 recipe quantity Cucumber & Tomato Raita (see page 172), to serve (optional)

Put the garlic and ginger in a mini food processor and process until a coarse paste forms, scraping down the side of the bowl as necessary. Leave to one side.

Melt 30g/1oz of the ghee in a large frying pan over a high heat. Reduce the heat to medium, add the lamb and fry for 3–5 minutes until browned on all sides, working in batches to avoid overcrowding the pan and adding extra ghee to the pan, if necessary. Use a slotted spoon to transfer the lamb to the slow cooker.

Melt the remaining ghee in the pan. Add the onions and fry, stirring, for 2 minutes. Add the garlic and ginger paste and fry for a further 1–3 minutes until the onion is softened.

Add the spices and cook, stirring, for 1 minute until fragrant. Stir in the tomato purée and bay leaves and season with salt and pepper. Add the mixture to the cooker and stir in 2 tablespoons water. Stir well, making sure the lamb is completely coated in the mixture.

Cover the cooker with the lid and cook on LOW for 5½ hours until the lamb is tender. Stir well, then mix together the yogurt and 2 tablespoons of the cooking liquid in a bowl. Stir the yogurt mixture into the curry and sprinkle in the garam masala. Re-cover the cooker and cook for a further 30 minutes. Remove and discard the bay leaves and cinnamon sticks and add a little more salt and pepper, if you like. Sprinkle with coriander and serve with rice and Cucumber and Tomato Raita, if you like.

MIDDLE EASTERN LAMB WITH FIGS & HONEY

PREPARATION TIME: 20 minutes
COOKING TIME: 6 hours on LOW, plus 15 minutes on HIGH   **SERVES 4**

2 tbsp olive oil, plus extra if needed

1 fennel bulb, sliced

2 garlic cloves, chopped

1 tbsp ground coriander

2 tsp ground cumin

½ tsp ground cloves

a pinch of dried chilli flakes, or to taste (optional)

750g/1lb 10oz boneless lamb shoulder, trimmed of fat
and cut into large chunks

90g/3¼oz/heaped ½ cup dried figs, coarsely chopped

2 preserved lemons, sliced

1 tbsp clear honey

lamb bones (optional), (you can ask your butcher
for these)

4 fresh figs, quartered

1–2 tbsp lemon or lime juice (optional)

salt and freshly ground black pepper

chopped coriander leaves, to serve

finely grated lemon or lime zest, to serve

2 tbsp sesame seeds, toasted (see page 170), to serve

flatbread, to serve

Heat 1 tablespoon of the oil in a large frying pan over a high heat. Reduce the heat to medium, add the fennel and fry, stirring, for 2 minutes. Add the garlic and spices and fry for a further 2 minutes. Transfer the mixture to the slow cooker, then wipe the pan with kitchen paper.

Heat the remaining oil in the pan. Add the lamb and fry for 3–5 minutes until browned on all sides, working in batches to avoid overcrowding the pan and adding extra oil, if necessary. Use a slotted spoon to transfer the lamb to the cooker.

Add the dried figs, preserved lemons, honey and lamb bones, if using, to the cooker. Pour over 185ml/6fl oz/¾ cup boiling water, stirring to dissolve the honey, then season with salt and pepper.

Cover the cooker with the lid and cook on LOW for 6 hours until the lamb is tender. Use a slotted spoon to remove the lamb from the cooker. Wrap in foil and leave to rest for about 10 minutes. Meanwhile, remove and discard the preserved lemons and lamb bones, if necessary. Skim any excess fat from the cooking liquid, then add the fresh figs. Switch the cooker to HIGH, re-cover and cook for 15 minutes until the figs are tender but still retain their shape.

Return the lamb and any cooking juices to the cooker and gently stir into the sauce. Add a little more salt and pepper and the lemon juice, if you like. Sprinkle the coriander, lemon zest and toasted sesame seeds over the lamb and figs and serve with flatbread.

FRENCH LAMB & FLAGEOLET BEANS

PREPARATION: 20 minutes, plus making the stock (optional)
COOKING TIME: 8¼ hours on LOW   **SERVES 4**

2 large garlic cloves, peeled

900g/2lb boneless lamb shoulder, rolled and tied

4 rosemary sprigs

2 tbsp garlic-infused olive oil

2 shallots, finely chopped

500ml/17fl oz/2 cups full-bodied dry red wine

250ml/9fl oz/1 cup Vegetable Stock (see page 169) or ready-made stock, plus extra if needed

2 bay leaves

800g/1lb 12oz tinned flageolet beans, drained and rinsed

salt and freshly ground black pepper

sautéed potatoes, to serve

Put the garlic on a chopping board, lightly sprinkle with salt and use the tip of a knife to crush into a paste. Using a small, sharp knife, make thin, deep slits all over the lamb, then use your fingers to push the garlic paste into the slits. Push one of the rosemary sprigs and any remaining garlic paste into the centre of the rolled lamb.

Heat the oil in a large frying pan over a high heat. Reduce the heat to medium, add the lamb and fry for 5–8 minutes until browned all over. Transfer the lamb to the slow cooker.

Pour off any excess fat from the pan, leaving about 1 tablespoon. Add the shallots and fry, stirring, for 2–3 minutes until golden. Add the wine, stock, bay leaves and remaining rosemary sprigs and season with salt and pepper. Bring to the boil, scraping the bottom of the pan, and boil until reduced by one-third. Pour the mixture into the cooker. The lamb will not be completely covered with liquid.

Cover the cooker with the lid and cook on LOW for 6 hours. Turn the lamb over, using tongs. Add the beans and stir well. The beans will not be completely covered with liquid. Re-cover the cooker as quickly as possible and cook for a further 2¼ hours until the lamb is cooked through and tender.

Remove the lamb from the cooker, wrap in foil and leave to rest for 10 minutes. Meanwhile, remove and discard the rosemary and bay leaves, and season with a little more salt and pepper, if you like. Re-cover the cooker to keep the beans warm. Carve the lamb and serve with the beans and cooking juices, and with sautéed potatoes.

TUSCAN LAMB SHANKS & BUTTER BEANS

PREPARATION TIME: 30 minutes, plus making the stock (optional)
COOKING TIME: 10 hours on LOW **SERVES 4**

4 lamb shanks, about 400g/14oz each

2 tbsp olive oil, plus extra if needed

2 carrots, finely chopped

1 celery stick, finely chopped

1 onion, finely chopped

6 large garlic cloves, finely chopped

750ml/26fl oz/3 cups dry red or white wine

250ml/9fl oz/1 cup Beef Stock (see page 168), Vegetable Stock (see page 169) or ready-made stock, plus extra if needed

2 bay leaves

leaves from 3 rosemary stalks and 1 tbsp dried sage, tied in a piece of muslin, plus extra chopped rosemary leaves, to serve

400g/14oz tinned butter beans, drained and rinsed

1 tsp balsamic vinegar, plus extra to taste

salt and freshly ground black pepper

Season the lamb shanks with salt and pepper. Heat the oil in a large frying pan over a high heat. Reduce the heat to medium, add the lamb shanks and fry for 5–8 minutes until browned on both sides, working in batches to avoid overcrowding the pan and adding extra oil to the pan, if necessary. Use tongs to transfer the lamb shanks to the slow cooker as they brown.

Pour off any excess fat from the pan, leaving about 1 tablespoon. Add the carrots, celery and onion and fry, stirring, for 2 minutes. Add the garlic and fry for a further 1–3 minutes until the onion is softened.

Add the wine, stock, bay leaves and herb bundle and season with salt and pepper. Bring to the boil, scraping the bottom of the pan, and boil until the liquid is reduced by half. Pour the mixture into the cooker. The lamb shanks will not be completely covered with liquid. Push the bay leaves and herb bundle down among the shanks.

Cover the cooker with the lid and cook on LOW for 6 hours. Remove the lamb shanks from the cooker, then stir the beans into the cooking liquid. Return the meat to the cooker, adding the shanks that were previously near the top of the cooker first. Re-cover the cooker as quickly as possible and cook for a further 4 hours until the lamb is tender and the beans are hot.

Remove and discard the bay leaves and herb bundle. Stir in the vinegar and add a little more salt, pepper and vinegar, if you like. Serve the lamb, beans and cooking liquid sprinkled with rosemary.

GREEK LAMB SHANKS IN TOMATO & GARLIC SAUCE

PREPARATION TIME: 15 minutes
COOKING TIME: 10 hours on LOW   **SERVES 4**

4 lamb shanks, about 400g/14oz each

2 tbsp dried oregano

670ml/23fl oz/2⅔ cups passata

1 large head of garlic, separated into cloves and peeled

1 large onion, finely chopped

1 red pepper, halved lengthways, deseeded and sliced

salt and freshly ground black pepper

oregano or coriander leaves, to serve

55g/2oz feta cheese, drained and crumbled, to serve

2 tbsp pine nuts, toasted (see page 170), to serve

sautéed potatoes, to serve

Season the lamb shanks with salt and pepper and put them in the slow cooker. Sprinkle over the dried oregano. Pour over the passata, using a spoon to smooth it over the exposed part of the lamb shanks. The lamb will not be completely covered with liquid. Push the garlic down between the lamb shanks, then push in the onion and pepper and season lightly with salt and pepper.

Cover the cooker with the lid. Cook on LOW for 10 hours until the lamb is tender and starting to fall off the bones.

Transfer the lamb shanks and pepper slices to shallow bowls. Use a wooden spoon to smash the garlic into the side of the container and stir into the sauce. Add a little more salt and pepper, if you like. Spoon the sauce over the lamb shanks. Sprinkle with oregano, feta and toasted pine nuts and serve with sautéed potatoes.

CLASSIC BEEF STEW WITH CHEESE & HERB DUMPLINGS

PREPARATION TIME: 25 minutes, plus making the stock (optional) and dumplings
COOKING TIME: 4½ hours on HIGH   **SERVES 4**

600g/1lb 5oz mixed root vegetables, such as carrots, celeriac, parsnip or swede, chopped

1 floury potato, such as Desiree, King Edward and Maris Piper, about 200g/7oz, chopped

2 bay leaves, torn

1 tbsp dried thyme or dried parsley

750g/1lb 10oz beef chuck or other stewing beef, trimmed of fat and cut into large chunks

2 tbsp plain white flour

1 tbsp dry mustard powder

2 tbsp sunflower oil, plus extra if needed

1 celery stick, thinly sliced

1 onion, chopped

4 garlic cloves, finely chopped

800ml/28fl oz/scant 3½ cups Beef Stock (see page 168) or ready-made stock, plus extra if needed

2 tbsp Worcestershire sauce

1 recipe quantity Cheese & Herb Dumplings (see page 169)

4 tbsp cornflour (optional)

salt and freshly ground black pepper

chopped parsley leaves, to serve

Put the root vegetables, potato, bay leaves and thyme in the slow cooker. Put the beef in a bowl and season with salt and pepper. Add the flour and mustard powder. Toss gently, making sure the beef is coated in the flour mixture. Shake off and reserve any excess mixture.

Heat the oil in a large frying pan over a high heat. Reduce the heat to medium, add the beef and fry for 5–8 minutes until browned on all sides, working in batches to avoid overcrowding the pan and adding extra oil, if necessary. Use a slotted spoon to transfer the beef to the cooker, then sprinkle over the reserved flour mixture.

Pour off any excess fat from the pan, leaving about 1 tablespoon. Add the celery and onion and fry, stirring, for 2 minutes. Add the garlic and fry for a further 1–3 minutes until the onion is softened. Add the stock and Worcestershire sauce and bring to the boil, scraping the bottom of the pan, then pour the mixture into the cooker and season.

Cover the cooker with the lid and cook on HIGH for 3½ hours. Quickly add the dumplings – they will sink, but rise to the surface as they cook. For a slightly thicker stew, put the cornflour in a bowl and stir in 2 tablespoons cold water until smooth. Stir the cornflour paste into the cooking liquid, then re-cover the cooker as quickly as possible and cook for 1 hour until the dumplings have risen and are cooked through. Discard the bay leaves and add more salt and pepper, if you like. Serve sprinkled with parsley.

GREEK SPICED BEEF & ONION STEW

When you look down the list of ingredients, you might think some stock has been missed off the list, but it hasn't. The small amount of added liquid and the cooking juices combine to make a thick, fragrant sauce.

PREPARATION TIME: 25 minutes
COOKING TIME: 7 hours on LOW   **SERVES 4**

4 tbsp olive oil, plus extra if needed

450g/1lb shallots or baby onions, peeled and an 'X' cut in the base of each

4 large garlic cloves, halved

750g/1lb 10oz boneless beef leg, trimmed of fat and cut into large chunks

4 bay leaves

3 cinnamon sticks

¼ tsp ground cloves

¼ tsp ground nutmeg, or to taste

2 tbsp red wine vinegar

450g/1lb tomatoes, grated and skins discarded

4 tbsp tomato purée

a pinch of caster sugar

salt and freshly ground black pepper

chopped mint or coriander leaves, to serve

boiled potatoes, to serve

Heat 2 tablespoons of the oil in a large frying pan over a high heat. Reduce the heat to medium, add the shallots and fry, stirring, for 3–5 minutes until just starting to turn golden. Add the garlic and stir for a further 1–2 minutes. Use a slotted spoon to transfer the shallots and garlic to the slow cooker.

Heat the remaining oil in the pan. Add the beef and fry for 3–5 minutes until browned, working in batches to avoid overcrowding the pan and adding extra oil, if necessary. Transfer the beef to the cooker.

Just before the final batch of beef finishes browning, add the bay leaves, cinnamon sticks, cloves and nutmeg and stir for 30 seconds until fragrant. Add the the vinegar and tomatoes and stir until the vinegar evaporates.

Transfer the beef mixture to the cooker. Put the tomato purée and 4 tablespoons water in a small bowl and stir until dissolved, then stir into the beef mixture. Stir in the sugar and season with salt and pepper. The beef and onions will not be completely covered with liquid.

Cover the cooker with the lid and cook on LOW for 7 hours until the beef is tender. Remove and discard the bay leaves and cinnamon sticks, and add a little more salt and pepper, if you like. Serve sprinkled with mint, and with boiled potatoes.

IRAQI BEEF DAUBE

PREPARATION TIME: 10 minutes, plus making
   the stock (optional)
COOKING TIME: 5 hours on HIGH   **SERVES 4**

750g/1lb 10oz piece of chuck steak, tied
8 allspice berries or ½ tsp ground allspice, or to taste
6 cloves
6 large garlic cloves, sliced lengthways
2 dried limes, slit open on one side
8 black peppercorns, very lightly crushed
1 cinnamon stick
500ml/17fl oz/2 cups passata
125ml/4fl oz/½ cup Beef Stock (see page 168)
   or ready-made stock
salt and freshly ground black pepper
chopped coriander leaves, to serve
pilaff, to serve (optional)

Make deep slits all over the beef and push the
allspice berries, cloves and garlic into the slits.

Put the beef in the slow cooker with the dried
limes, peppercorns and cinnamon stick. Add the
passata and stock and season with salt and pepper.

Cover the cooker with the lid and cook on HIGH for
5 hours until the beef is tender. Remove the beef,
wrap in foil and leave to rest for 5 minutes.

Meanwhile, remove and discard the cinnamon
stick and dried limes and add a little more salt and
pepper, if you like. Re-cover the cooker to keep the
sauce warm.

Slice the beef, then sprinkle with coriander and
serve with the cooking liquid spooned over the top,
and with pilaff, if you like.

ONE-STEP BEEF STEW

PREPARATION TIME: 10 minutes
COOKING TIME: 10 hours on LOW   **SERVES 4**

600g/1lb 5oz butternut squash, peeled, deseeded and
   cut into large chunks
250g/9oz waxy potatoes, such as Charlotte, Jersey
   Royals and new potatoes, scrubbed and chopped
1 fennel head, chopped
1 onion, chopped
4 garlic cloves, chopped
2 tbsp dried thyme
700g/1lb 9oz boneless beef shin, cut into large chunks
400g/14oz/scant 1⅔ cups tinned chopped tomatoes
2 tbsp tomato purée
2 bay leaves, torn
salt and freshly ground black pepper
chopped parsley leaves, to serve

Put the squash, potatoes, fennel, onion, garlic and
thyme in the slow cooker. Add the beef, chopped
tomatoes and tomato purée, then tuck the bay
leaves among the pieces of beef. Spoon over
4 tablespoons water and season with salt and
pepper. The ingredients will not be completely
covered with liquid.

Cover the cooker with the lid and cook on LOW for
10 hours.

Remove and discard the bay leaves. Add more salt
and pepper, if you like. Serve sprinkled with parsley.

BEEF BORSCHT

PREPARATION TIME: 15 minutes
COOKING TIME: 11½ hours on LOW,
 plus 30 minutes on HIGH   **SERVES 4**

750g/1lb 10oz piece of boneless beef shin
4 tsp caraway seeds
2 large tomatoes, chopped
4 bay leaves
4 large raw beetroot, peeled and halved
4 garlic cloves, crushed
2 celery sticks, chopped
2 onions, chopped
2 carrots, 1 chopped and 1 grated
4 tbsp red wine vinegar, plus extra to taste
2 tbsp soft light brown sugar, plus extra to taste
2 tbsp tomato purée
100g/3½oz white cabbage, cored and shredded
salt and freshly ground black pepper

Put the beef, seeds, tomatoes, bay leaves, beetroot, garlic, celery, onions, chopped carrot, vinegar, sugar and tomato purée in the slow cooker and season. Pour over 1l/35fl oz/4 cups boiling water, stirring. All the vegetables might not be covered with water.

Cover the cooker with the lid and cook on LOW for 11½ hours until the beef is tender. Remove the beef from the cooker and leave to cool slightly.

Strain the cooking liquid into a bowl, pressing down on the vegetables. Discard the solids. Skim any excess fat from the the cooking liquid. Return the liquid to the cooker and add the cabbage and grated carrot. Switch the cooker to HIGH, re-cover and cook for 30 minutes until the vegetables are tender. When the meat is cool enough to handle, remove and discard the skin and any gristle, then thinly slice and keep warm. When the vegetables are tender, add a little more vinegar or sugar, if you like. Serve with the beef.

BARBECUED BEEF SANDWICHES

PREPARATION TIME: 5 minutes, plus making the
 barbecue sauce (optional)
COOKING TIME: 10 hours on LOW
MAKES 8 SANDWICHES

700g/1lb 9oz boneless beef chuck or other stewing
 beef, cut into large chunks
250ml/9fl oz/1 cup Barbecue Sauce (see page 33)
 or bottled sauce of your choice
1 dill pickle, quartered lengthways
salt and freshly ground black pepper
8 hamburger buns, cut in half, to serve
crisps, to serve (optional)

Put the beef, barbecue sauce and dill pickle in the slow cooker and season with salt and pepper, then stir the ingredients together.

Cover the cooker with the lid and cook on LOW for 10 hours. Remove and discard the dill pickle quarters. Use a slotted spoon to remove the beef from the cooker, leaving behind as much sauce as possible. Leave the beef to rest for 5 minutes. Re-cover the cooker to keep the sauce warm.

Use two forks to shred the beef, then return the meat to the sauce and stir until combined. Serve hot or at room temperature, spooned on to hamburger buns, and with crisps, if you like.

BEEF BURRITOS

PREPARATION TIME: 20 minutes
COOKING TIME: 10 hours on Low   **SERVES 4**

4 large garlic cloves, peeled

1 tbsp dried oregano

1 tbsp sweet paprika

1 tbsp ground cumin

2 tsp ground coriander

2 tbsp sunflower oil

700g/1lb 9oz skirt steak, halved lengthways, then quartered

450g/1lb tomatoes, coarsely chopped

2 red peppers, halved lengthways, deseeded and coarsely chopped

4 tbsp passata

1 tsp hot pickled jalapeño chillies, or to taste

several coriander sprigs, leaves and stalks separated, with the stalks tied together

1 bay leaf

8 flour tortillas

salt and freshly ground black pepper

FILLINGS (OPTIONAL)

coarsely grated Cheddar or Monterey Jack cheese

pitted black olives, sliced

skinned and deseeded tomatoes, thinly sliced

shredded cos lettuce

Put the garlic on a chopping board, lightly sprinkle with salt and use the tip of a knife to crush into a paste. Transfer the paste to a small bowl and stir in the oregano, paprika, cumin, ground coriander and oil. Use your hands to rub the mixture all over the pieces of steak, then season with salt and pepper.

Put the tomatoes, peppers, passata, pickled chillies, coriander stalks and bay leaf in the slow cooker and top with the pieces of steak.

Cover the cooker with the lid and cook on LOW for 10 hours until the meat is very tender. Remove the steak from the cooker, wrap in foil and leave to rest for at least 10 minutes. Remove and discard the bay leaf and coriander stalks. Re-cover the cooker to keep the sauce warm.

Meanwhile, preheat the oven to 180°C/350°F/Gas 4. Wrap the tortillas in foil and heat in the oven for 10–15 minutes until hot. (Alternatively, wrap in cling film and warm in a microwave on HIGH for 30–45 seconds.)

Use two forks to shred the steak, then stir the meat into the sauce and season with a little more salt and pepper, if you like.

To assemble a burrito, spoon the beef filling down the centre of one tortilla, using a slotted spoon. Add any or all of the toppings, if you like, and sprinkle with coriander leaves. Roll up the tortilla, then repeat to make 7 more burritos. Serve hot.

NEW ENGLAND POT ROAST

PREPARATION TIME: 20 minutes, plus making the stock and cream (optional)
COOKING TIME: 2 hours on HIGH, plus 8 hours on LOW   **SERVES 4**

1kg/2lb 4oz boneless beef brisket or silverside, rolled and tied

2 tbsp plain white flour

2 tbsp sunflower oil

8 new potatoes, scrubbed and halved or quartered, if large

4 large garlic cloves, finely chopped

2 bay leaves

2 red onions, sliced

2 large carrots, sliced

2 swedes, quartered

250ml/9fl oz/1 cup Beef Stock (see page 168) or ready-made stock

salt and freshly ground black pepper

1 recipe quantity Horseradish & Dill Cream (see page 173), to serve (optional)

Season the brisket with salt and pepper, then use your hands to rub the flour all over the meat. Heat the oil in a large frying pan over a high heat. Reduce the heat to medium, add the brisket and fry for 5–8 minutes, turning once, until browned all over.

Transfer the brisket to the slow cooker, then add the potatoes, garlic, bay leaves, red onions, carrots and swedes. Pour over the stock and season lightly with salt and pepper. The vegetables will not be completely covered with liquid.

Cover the cooker with the lid. Cook on HIGH for 2 hours, then switch the cooker to LOW and cook for a further 8 hours until the beef and vegetables are tender. Transfer the brisket, potatoes, carrots and swedes to a large plate, then cover with foil to keep warm and leave the brisket to rest for about 10 minutes.

Meanwhile, strain the cooking liquid into a small saucepan, pressing down on the onions to extract as much flavour as possible. Bring to the boil over a high heat. Boil for 5 minutes until slightly reduced and the flavours have concentrated. Add a little more salt and pepper, if you like.

Carve the brisket, then spoon the onion sauce over the brisket and vegetables and serve with Horseradish and Dill Cream, if you like.

GERMAN SAUERBRATEN

PREPARATION TIME: 40 minutes, plus cooling, 3–4 days marinating, and making the stock (optional)
COOKING TIME: 2¼ hours on HIGH, plus 7¾ hours on LOW   **SERVES 4**

1 kg/2lb 4oz boneless beef brisket, not rolled

4 tbsp plain white flour

2 tbsp sunflower oil

2 onions, chopped

1 carrot, chopped

1 celery stick, chopped

350ml/12fl oz/scant 1½ cups Beef Stock (see page 168) or ready-made stock

8 gingernut biscuits, crumbled

salt and freshly ground black pepper

mashed potatoes, to serve

red cabbage cooked with apples, to serve

MARINADE

450ml/16fl oz/scant 2 cups dry red wine

125ml/4fl oz/½ cup red wine vinegar

2 onions, sliced

1 carrot, sliced

8 juniper berries, lightly crushed

8 allspice berries, lightly crushed, or ½ tsp ground allspice

8 black peppercorns, lightly crushed

8 cloves

2 bay leaves

To make the marinade, put all of the ingredients in a saucepan with 125ml/4fl oz/½ cup water. Bring to the boil over a high heat, then reduce the heat to low and simmer for 15 minutes. Leave to cool completely. Put the brisket in a non-metallic bowl and pour over the marinade. Cover and marinate in the fridge for 3–4 days, turning the meat twice a day.

Remove the beef from the marinade and reserve the marinade. Pat the beef dry, season with salt and pepper and rub 2 tablespoons of the flour all over the meat. Heat the oil in a frying pan over a high heat. Reduce the heat to medium, add the brisket and fry for 3–5 minutes until browned. Transfer to the slow cooker.

Pour off any excess fat in the pan, leaving about 1 tablespoon. Add the onions, carrot and celery and fry, stirring, for 3–5 minutes until the onion is softened. Transfer the vegetables to the cooker. Strain the reserved marinade into the pan, discarding the solids. Add the stock and bring to the boil, then boil until reduced by half. Pour over the brisket.

Cover the cooker with the lid and cook on HIGH for 2 hours, then switch the cooker to LOW and cook for 7¾ hours until the beef is tender. Remove the beef, cover and keep warm. Put the remaining flour and 4 tablespoons of the cooking liquid in a small bowl and stir until smooth. Stir the paste into the cooking liquid with the gingersnaps. Switch the cooker to HIGH, re-cover and cook for 15 minutes until thick, then stir. Carve the beef. Strain the sauce, pressing down firmly on the vegetables, then discard the solids. Spoon the sauce over the beef and serve with mashed potatoes and red cabbage.

CUBAN ROPA VIEJA

Flank steak is the ideal cut for this rich stew. The recipe is called 'old clothes', because the tender, succulent steak is shredded like rags just before serving.

PREPARATION TIME: 15 minutes
COOKING TIME: 10 hours on LOW   **SERVES 4**

700g/1lb 9oz flank steak, halved lengthways, then quartered

2 tbsp olive oil

2 green peppers, halved lengthways, deseeded and sliced

1 large onion, sliced

4 large garlic cloves, chopped

2 tsp ground cumin

1 tsp ground cinnamon

a pinch of ground cloves

400g/14oz/scant 1⅔ cups tinned chopped tomatoes

2 tbsp tomato purée

1 bay leaf

1 habañero or other hot chilli, deseeded if you like, and thinly sliced

110g/3¾oz/½ cup green olives, pitted and sliced

2 tbsp drained capers in brine, rinsed

salt and freshly ground black pepper

chopped coriander leaves, to serve

cooked long-grain white rice, to serve

Season the steak with salt and pepper and leave to one side. Heat the oil in a large frying pan over a high heat. Reduce the heat to medium, add the peppers and onion and fry, stirring, for 2 minutes. Add the garlic, cumin, cinnamon and cloves and stir for a further 1–2 minutes until the onions are softened.

Add the chopped tomatoes, tomato purée, bay leaf and chilli and season lightly with salt and pepper. Bring to the boil, stirring, then pour the mixture into the slow cooker and top with the pieces of steak.

Cover the cooker with the lid and cook on LOW for 10 hours until the meat is very tender. Remove the steak from the cooker, wrap in foil and leave to rest for 10 minutes. Meanwhile, remove and discard the bay leaf, then add the olives and capers to the sauce. Re-cover the cooker and heat through.

Use two forks to shred the beef, then stir the meat into the sauce and add a little more salt and pepper, if you like. Sprinkle with coriander and serve with rice.

TWO-COURSE ITALIAN BEEF

Beef shin is one of those underrated, inexpensive cuts perfectly transformed by the slow cooker. It's an ideal choice for this Italian-inspired two-course meal.

PREPARATION TIME: 10 minutes, plus making the salsa verde
COOKING TIME: 1¼ hours on HIGH, plus 8¾ hours on LOW   **SERVES 4**

750g/1lb 10oz boneless beef shin, tied lengthways

2 bay leaves, torn

2 fennel bulbs, quartered

1 celery stick with leaves, quartered

1 large onion, quartered

1 tbsp fennel seeds

4 tbsp small soup pasta, such as stars or loops

salt and freshly ground black pepper

freshly grated Parmesan cheese, to serve

1 recipe quantity Salsa Verde (see page 174), to serve

salad, to serve

Put the beef, bay leaves, fennel, celery, onion and fennel seeds in the slow cooker, tucking the vegetables down around the beef, if necessary. Fill the container with water, leaving a 2.5cm/1in gap at the top of the pot, and season with salt and pepper.

Cover the cooker with the lid. Cook on HIGH for 1 hour, then switch the cooker to LOW and cook for a further 8¾ hours until the beef is tender.

When the beef is almost tender, preheat the oven to 150°C/300°F/Gas 2. Use a large metal spoon to skim any excess fat from the surface of the cooking liquid. When the beef is tender, transfer to a rimmed heatproof plate and ladle enough cooking liquid over the top to keep the meat moist. Cover with foil and keep warm in the oven until required.

Strain the cooking liquid into a bowl, reserving the fennel and discarding the other solids, then return the liquid to the cooker and switch the cooker to HIGH. Finely chop the cooked fennel. Add the fennel and pasta to the cooker, then season with a little more salt and pepper, if you like.

Re-cover the cooker and cook for a futher 15 minutes until the pasta is tender. Serve the broth, fennel and pasta as a first course sprinkled with grated Parmesan. For a second course, thinly slice the beef and serve with Salsa Verde and salad.

BEEF & AUBERGINE TAGINE

This is a very rich and filling dish. When friends come round for dinner,
I simply serve it with a bowl of couscous, followed by fruit. Orange slices dusted
with ground ginger and ground cardamom are especially good.

PREPARATION TIME: 25 minutes, plus making the stock (optional)
COOKING TIME: 7 hours on LOW   **SERVES 4**

750g/1lb 10oz boneless beef shoulder, trimmed of fat and cut into large chunks

2 tbsp olive oil, plus extra if needed

350g/12oz aubergine, peeled and chopped

8 dates or ready-to-eat dried apricots

2 preserved lemons, sliced

1 fennel bulb, sliced

4 large garlic cloves, finely chopped

2 bay leaves

2 tsp fennel seeds

1 tbsp ground cumin

1 tbsp ras el hanout

2 tsp dried thyme

2 tbsp tomato purée

250ml/9fl oz/1 cup Beef Stock (see page 168), ready-made stock or water

salt and freshly ground black pepper

chopped coriander leaves, to serve

pomegranate seeds (optional), to serve

cooked couscous, to serve

Season the beef with salt and pepper. Heat the oil in a large frying pan over a high heat. Reduce the heat to medium, add the beef and fry for 3–5 minutes until browned on all sides, working in batches to avoid overcrowding the pan and adding extra oil, if necessary. Use a slotted spoon to transfer the beef to the slow cooker, then add the aubergine, dates and preserved lemons.

Pour off any excess fat from the pan, leaving about 1 tablespoon. Add the fennel and fry, stirring, for 2 minutes. Add the garlic and fry for a further 1–3 minutes until the fennel is softened. Add the bay leaves, fennel seeds, cumin, ras el hanout and thyme and fry for 30–60 seconds until fragrant.

Add the tomato purée and stock and season lightly with salt and pepper. Bring to the boil, stirring, then pour the mixture into the cooker and stir well.

Cover the cooker with the lid and cook on LOW for 7 hours until the beef is tender. Remove and discard the bay leaves, then stir well and add a little more salt and pepper, if you like. Sprinkle with coriander and pomegranate seeds, if you like, and serve with couscous.

MASSAMAN BEEF & POTATO CURRY

One of the reasons I like making this fragrant, soup-like Thai curry is that it really is a complete meal-in-a-pot. It contains potatoes, so I don't even have to think about cooking any rice.

PREPARATION TIME: 10 minutes, plus making the curry paste, and stock (optional)
COOKING TIME: 8 hours on LOW   **SERVES 4**

280g/10oz small new potatoes, peeled and halved if large

750g/1lb 10oz boneless beef leg, trimmed of fat and cut into large chunks

250g/9oz Thai or small shallots, peeled

250g/9oz green beans, trimmed

1 recipe quantity Massaman Curry Paste (see page 170)

125ml/4fl oz/½ cup Beef Stock (see page 168) or ready-made stock, boiling

250ml/9fl oz/1 cup coconut milk

1 kaffir lime leaf

salt and freshly ground black pepper

chopped coriander leaves, to serve

chopped salted peanuts, to serve

Put the potatoes in the slow cooker, then add the beef, shallots and green beans.

Dissolve the curry paste in the stock, then pour it over the beef and vegetables. Pour over the coconut milk, add the lime leaf, season with salt and pepper and stir. The beef and vegetables will not be completely covered with liquid.

Cover the cooker with the lid and cook on LOW for 8 hours until the beef and vegetables are tender. Add a little more salt and pepper, if you like. Sprinkle with coriander and peanuts and serve.

BOBOTIE

PREPARATION TIME: 25 minutes, plus 10 minutes standing
COOKING TIME: 2 hours on LOW, plus 1 hour on HIGH   **SERVES 4**

55g/2oz/½ cup dried breadcrumbs

2 tbsp sunflower oil

1 onion, finely chopped

4 large garlic cloves, finely chopped

1 tbsp Madras curry powder, or to taste

2 tsp ground mixed spice

1 tbsp dried mixed herbs

700g/1lb 9oz lean minced beef, or a mixture of minced beef and minced lamb

100g/3½oz/heaped ½ cup ready-to-eat dried apricots, halved

3 bay leaves

1 green chilli, deseeded and finely chopped (optional)

4 tbsp sultanas or raisins

finely grated zest of 1 large lemon

salt and freshly ground black pepper

TOPPING

2 large eggs

300ml/10½fl oz/scant 1¼ cups milk

¼ tsp turmeric

salt

Put the breadcrumbs in a bowl, add just enough water to cover and leave to soak. Meanwhile, heat 1 tablespoon of the oil in a large frying pan over a high heat. Reduce the heat to medium, add the onion and fry, stirring, for 2 minutes. Add the garlic, curry powder and mixed spice and fry for a further 1–3 minutes until the onion is softened. Use a slotted spoon to transfer the mixture to the slow cooker, then sprinkle with the mixed herbs.

Heat the remaining oil in the pan. Add the beef and fry, breaking up the meat, until browned all over. Use a slotted spoon to transfer the beef to the cooker, leaving behind as much oil as possible. Add the dried apricots, bay leaves, chilli, if using, sultanas and lemon zest to the cooker and season with salt and pepper. Squeeze the breadcrumbs to remove as much water as possible, then add to the cooker and stir well. Cover with the lid and cook on LOW for 2 hours.

Five minutes before the end of the cooking time, make the topping. Mix all of the ingredients in a bowl and season with salt. Remove the cooker lid and stir the beef mixture. Skim any excess fat from the cooking liquid, then remove and discard the bay leaves. Add a little more salt and pepper, if you like, then pour over the topping mixture.

Quickly cover the top of the slow cooker with cling film and re-cover with the lid. Switch the cooker to HIGH and cook for a further 1 hour until the topping is set. Remove the cling film and leave the bobotie to stand for 10 minutes until the topping firms up. Serve straight from the container.

CURRIED MINCE & PEAS

PREPARATION TIME: 20 minutes, plus making the stock and raita (optional)
COOKING TIME: 4 hours on LOW, plus 15 minutes on HIGH   **SERVES 4**

2 tbsp sunflower oil

2 cinnamon sticks

1 onion, finely chopped

4cm/1½in piece of root ginger, peeled and finely chopped

4 garlic cloves, finely chopped

2 green chillies, deseeded and finely chopped

1 tbsp curry powder

2 tsp ground cardamom

1 tsp ground coriander

1 tsp ground cumin

½ tsp ground cloves

¼ tsp cayenne pepper, or to taste

¼ tsp turmeric

700g/1lb 9oz lean minced beef

400g/14oz/scant 1⅔ cups tinned chopped tomatoes

4 tbsp passata

125ml/4fl oz/½ cup Beef Stock (see page 168), Vegetable Stock (see page 169) or ready-made stock

1 bay leaf

200g/7oz/1⅓ cups frozen peas, defrosted

salt and freshly ground black pepper

chopped coriander leaves, to serve

warm naan breads, to serve

1 recipe quantity Cucumber & Tomato Raita (see page 172), to serve (optional)

Heat 1 tablespoon of the oil in a large frying pan over a medium-high heat. Add the cinnamon sticks and fry, stirring, for about 30 seconds until fragrant. Use a slotted spoon to remove the cinnamon sticks from the pan and leave to one side.

Reduce the heat to medium. Add the onion to the pan and fry for 2 minutes. Add the ginger, garlic, chillies, curry powder and spices and fry for a further 1–3 minutes until the onion is softened. Use a slotted spoon to transfer the mixture to the slow cooker.

Heat the remaining oil in the pan. Add the beef and fry, breaking up the meat, until browned all over. Use a slotted spoon to transfer the beef to the cooker, leaving behind as much oil as possible. Add the chopped tomatoes, passata, stock, bay leaf and fried cinnamon sticks to the cooker and stir well, then season with salt and pepper.

Cover the cooker with the lid and cook on LOW for 4 hours, then stir in the peas. Switch the cooker to HIGH, re-cover and cook for 15 minutes until the peas are tender. Remove and discard the bay leaf and cinnamon sticks and add a little more salt and pepper, if you like. Sprinkle with coriander and serve with naan breads and Cucumber and Tomato Raita, if you like.

RIBS BRAISED IN RED WINE

PREPARATION TIME: 30 minutes, plus making the stock (optional)
COOKING TIME: 9 hours on LOW   **SERVES 4**

1.6kg/3lb 8oz bone-in beef short ribs in large pieces

2 tbsp olive oil, plus extra if needed

2 carrots, chopped

1 celery stick, finely chopped

1 onion, chopped

500ml/17fl oz/2 cups Beef Stock (see page 168) or ready-made stock

750ml/26fl oz/3 cups full-bodied red wine

8 black peppercorns, crushed

6 garlic cloves, finely chopped

2 bay leaves, torn

3 tbsp herbes de Provence or dried mixed herbs

40g/1½oz butter, softened

3 tbsp plain white flour

salt and freshly ground black pepper

mashed potatoes, to serve (optional)

Season the ribs with salt and pepper. Heat the oil in a large frying pan over a high heat. Reduce the heat to medium, add the ribs and fry until browned on all sides, working in batches to avoid overcrowding the pan and adding extra oil, if necessary. Transfer the ribs to the slow cooker as they brown

Pour off any excess fat from the pan, leaving about 1 tablespoon. Add the carrots, celery and onion and fry, stirring, for 3–5 minutes until the onion is softened. Add the stock, wine, peppercorns, garlic, bay leaves and herbs and season with salt and pepper. Bring to the boil, stirring, until the liquid is reduced by half. Pour the mixture into the cooker. The ribs will not be completely covered with liquid.

Cover the cooker with the lid. Cook on LOW for 9 hours until the meat and vegetables are tender and the meat comes away from the bones easily. Remove the meat from the cooker, then wrap in foil and keep warm. Discard any bones and the bay leaves.

Beat together the butter and flour. Strain the cooking liquid through a fine sieve into a saucepan, pressing down to extract as much flavour as possible. Skim any excess fat from the cooking liquid, and bring to the boil. Gradually whisk in the butter mixture. Boil, whisking continuously, over a high heat for a further 5 minutes until the sauce reduces to about 500ml/17fl oz/2 cups and thickens. Add a little more salt and pepper, if you like. Serve the beef with the sauce spooned over the top, and with mashed potatoes, if you like.

KOREAN RIBS & DAIKON

The meat on the ribs takes on an extra dimension of flavour as it absorbs the sharp peppery flavour of the daikon. Cooking the slender white daikon in large chunks ensures it doesn't overcook, so it can be diced and served alongside the rich meat.

PREPARATION TIME: 15 minutes, plus pickling the bean sprouts (optional)
COOKING TIME: 5 hours on HIGH   **SERVES 4**

250ml/9fl oz/1 cup dark soy sauce
8 spring onions, finely chopped, plus extra to serve
5cm/2in piece of root ginger, finely grated
8 garlic cloves, very finely chopped
4 tbsp dark brown sugar
1 tbsp sesame oil
1.6 kg/3lb 8oz bone-in beef short ribs in large pieces
400g/14oz daikon, cut into thick pieces
salt and freshly ground black pepper
2 tbsp sesame seeds, toasted (see page 170), to serve
Pickled Bean Sprouts (see page 173) or kimchi, to serve

Put the soy sauce, spring onions, ginger, garlic, brown sugar, oil and 125ml/4fl oz/½ cup water in the slow cooker, stirring to dissolve the sugar. Season with pepper. Add the ribs and spoon the liquid over the top, making sure the ribs are coated in the soy sauce mixture. Add the daikon, tucking it down around the ribs. The ribs and daikon will not be completely covered with liquid.

Cover the cooker with the lid and cook on HIGH for 5 hours until the meat is tender and comes away from the bones easily.

When the meat is tender, season with salt, if needed, and add a little more pepper, if you like. Remove the daikon from the cooking liquid and dice it. Use a large metal spoon to skim any excess fat from the surface of the cooking liquid, and remove and discard any bones.

Spoon the cooking liquid over the meat, sprinkle with toasted sesame seeds and spring onions and serve with the daikon and Pickled Bean Sprouts.

SPANISH MEATBALLS

PREPARATION TIME: 30 minutes, plus making the tomato sauce (optional)
COOKING TIME: 4 hours on LOW, plus 15 minutes on HIGH **SERVES 4**

40g/1½oz/¼ cup pine nuts, toasted (see page 170)

250g/9oz lean minced beef

250g/9oz lean minced pork

55g/2oz/½ cup dried breadcrumbs

4 large garlic cloves, very finely chopped

2 eggs, beaten

3 tbsp finely chopped parsley leaves

¼ tsp ground cinnamon

3 tbsp plain white flour, for dusting, plus extra if needed

1 tbsp garlic-infused olive oil, plus extra if needed

280g/10oz/heaped 1¾ cups frozen peas, defrosted

salt and freshly ground black pepper

cooked short-grain white rice, to serve

SAUCE

1 large onion, finely chopped

4 large garlic cloves, crushed

350g/12oz cooking chorizo, skinned and diced

600ml/21fl oz/scant 2½ cups Easy Tomato Sauce (see page 34), bottled tomato sauce or passata

To make the meatballs, put the pine nuts, beef, pork, breadcrumbs, garlic, eggs, parsley and cinnamon in a bowl and season with salt and pepper. Combine the ingredients, using wet hands, making sure the pine nuts and parsley are evenly distributed. Divide the mixture into 2 equal portions, then roll each half into 10 balls. Transfer the meatballs to a floured plate.

Heat the oil in a frying pan over a high heat. Reduce the heat to medium, add the meatballs and fry for 3–5 minutes, until browned all over, working in batches and adding extra oil, if necessary. Transfer the meatballs to the slow cooker.

To make the sauce, pour off any excess fat from the pan, leaving about 1 tablespoon. Add the onion and fry, stirring, for 2 minutes. Add the garlic and chorizo and fry for a further 1–3 minutes until the onion is softened. Add the tomato sauce and bring to the boil, scraping the bottom of the pan, then pour the mixture into the cooker.

Cover the cooker and cook on LOW for 4 hours. Test the meatballs are cooked through by cutting one in half. Return the meatball to the cooker and add the peas. Switch the cooker to HIGH, re-cover and cook for 15 minutes until the peas are tender. Add a little more salt and pepper, if you like. Serve the meatballs and sauce spooned over rice.

COOK'S TIP
To check for seasoning in the meatballs, fry a small amount of the mixture before it is shaped and taste. This way you can add extra salt and/or pepper before the meatballs are fried.

ISRAELI SABBATH BRISKET

PREPARATION TIME: 30 minutes
COOKING TIME: 2 hours on HIGH, plus 8 hours on LOW   **SERVES 4**

700g/1lb 9oz brisket, cut into large chunks

2 tbsp olive oil, plus extra if needed

400g/14oz tinned red kidney beans, drained and rinsed

400g/14oz new potatoes, peeled and halved or quartered, if large

2 onions, chopped

4 garlic cloves, chopped

100g/3½oz/½ cup pearl barley

2 bay leaves

4 tbsp dark brown sugar

2 tbsp tomato purée

1 tbsp dried thyme

1½ tsp sweet, smoked or hot paprika, or to taste

4 eggs, at room temperature

salt and freshly ground black pepper

chopped parsley leaves, to serve

Season the brisket with salt and pepper. Heat the oil in a large frying pan over a high heat. Reduce the heat to medium, add the beef and fry for 3–5 minutes, until browned on all sides, working in batches to avoid overcrowding the pan and adding extra oil, if necessary. Use a slotted spoon to transfer the beef to the slow cooker. Add the beans and potatoes to the cooker.

Pour off any excess fat from the pan, leaving about 1 tablespoon. Reduce the heat to low, add the onions and fry, stirring, for 8–10 minutes until just starting to brown. Add the garlic and stir for 1 minute. Transfer the onions and garlic to the cooker.

Add the barley, bay leaves, brown sugar, tomato purée, thyme and paprika to the cooker and season lightly with salt and pepper. Pour over just enough boiling water to cover all of the ingredients, then stir to dissolve the sugar and tomato purée.

Cover the cooker with the lid and cook on HIGH for 2 hours, then switch the cooker to LOW and cook for a further 7 hours. Add the eggs, gently pushing them down into the cooking liquid. Re-cover the cooker and cook for another 1 hour until the meat, barley and potatoes are tender.

Remove and discard the bay leaves and add a little more salt and pepper, if you like. Remove the eggs from the cooker, then shell them. Divide the eggs into bowls, then add a mixture of meat, potatoes and barley to each. Sprinkle with parsley and serve.

IRISH OX CHEEKS

PREPARATION TIME: 25 minutes
COOKING TIME: 6 hours on LOW,
  plus 30 minutes on HIGH   **SERVES 4**

2 ox cheeks, about 500g/1lb 2oz each, trimmed of fat
  and cut into large pieces
2 tbsp plain white flour
1 tbsp sunflower oil
4 tbsp oat groats
6 juniper berries, tied in a piece of muslin and crushed
200g/7oz parsnips, peeled, cored and diced
350g/12oz leeks, halved lengthways, sliced and rinsed
2 large garlic cloves, chopped
330ml/11¼fl oz/1⅓ cups stout, ale or lager
200g/7oz white cabbage, cored and shredded
salt and freshly ground black pepper
boiled or mashed potatoes, to serve

Season the ox cheeks with salt and pepper and dust
with the flour. Heat the oil in a frying pan over a high
heat. Reduce the heat to medium, add the cheeks
and fry for 3–5 minutes until browned. Transfer to
the slow cooker. Add the oats and juniper bundle,
tucking them between the meat. Add the parsnips.

Pour off any excess fat from the pan, leaving about
1 tablespoon. Add the leeks and fry, stirring, for
2 minutes. Add the garlic and fry for a further 1–3
minutes. Transfer the leeks and garlic to the cooker,
then pour over the stout and season with pepper.

Cover the cooker and cook on LOW for 6 hours until
the beef is tender. Remove the meat, wrap in foil and
keep warm. Discard the juniper bundle, then skim
any excess fat from the cooking liquid. Switch the
cooker to HIGH and add the cabbage. Re-cover and
cook for 30 minutes until the oats are tender. Season
with salt and a little pepper, if you like. Cut the meat
into bite-sized pieces and serve with potatoes.

OXTAIL FARRO

PREPARATION TIME: 10 minutes,
  plus making the stock (optional)
COOKING TIME: 10 hours on LOW   **SERVES 4**

225g/8oz carrots, thickly sliced
150g/5½oz parsnips, peeled and cut into chunks
1 onion, finely chopped
2 tbsp dried sage or thyme
1.5kg/3lb 5oz oxtail, cut into chunks
600ml/21fl oz/scant 2½ cups Beef Stock (see page
  168) or ready-made stock
2 tbsp tomato purée
1 tbsp Worcestershire sauce, plus extra to taste
4 tbsp farro or pearl barley
salt and freshly ground black pepper
chopped parsley leaves, to serve
mashed potatoes, to serve

Put the carrots, parsnips and onion in the slow
cooker and sprinkle over the sage. Top with the
oxtail chunks. Pour over the stock, then stir in the
tomato purée and Worcestershire sauce and season
with pepper. Push the farro into the liquid, tucking
it down between the oxtail chunks. The oxtail will
not be completely covered with liquid.

Cover the cooker with the lid and cook on LOW for
10 hours until the meat is very tender and starting
to fall off the bones.

Remove and discard any bones. Season with salt
and add a little more Worcestershire sauce and
pepper, if you like. Divide the oxtail and vegetables
into bowls. Spoon over the farro and cooking liquid,
then sprinkle with parsley and serve with mashed
potatoes.

VEAL, FENNEL & RED PEPPER STEW

PREPARATION TIME: 25 minutes, plus making the stock and 20 minutes thickening time (optional)
COOKING TIME: 6½ hours on LOW   **SERVES 4**

750g/1lb 10oz boneless veal shoulder, trimmed of fat and cut into large chunks

2 tbsp plain white flour

2 tbsp olive oil, plus extra if needed

2 fennel bulbs, chopped with the fronds reserved

4 large garlic cloves, finely chopped

4 tbsp aniseed-flavoured spirit

250ml/9fl oz/1 cup Vegetable Stock (see page 169) or ready-made stock

1 tbsp dried dill

1 tbsp fennel seeds, tied in a piece of muslin and lightly crushed

4 large chargrilled, skinless red peppers in oil, drained and sliced

2 tbsp cornflour (optional)

salt and freshly ground black pepper

polenta or boiled potatoes, to serve

Put the the veal in a bowl and season with salt and pepper. Add the flour and toss gently, shaking off and reserving any excess flour. Heat the oil in a frying pan over a high heat. Reduce the heat to medium, add the veal and fry for 5–8 minutes until browned, working in batches and adding extra oil, if necessary. Transfer the veal to the slow cooker, then sprinkle over the reserved flour.

Pour off any excess fat from the pan, leaving about 1 tablespoon. Add the fennel and fry, stirring, for 2 minutes. Add the garlic and fry for 1–3 minutes until the fennel is softened. Add the spirit, then carefully set it alight and allow the flames to flare up and die out. Transfer the fennel to the cooker, then add the stock and dill and stir well. Push the fennel seed bundle down between the pieces of veal. Season lightly with salt and pepper. The ingredients will not be completely covered with liquid.

Cover the cooker with the lid and cook on LOW for 6 hours. Stir in the peppers. Re-cover the cooker and cook for a further 30 minutes until the veal is tender. Use a slotted spoon to remove the veal and vegetables from the cooker, then wrap in foil and keep warm.

For a thicker sauce, put the cornflour and 4 tablespoons cold water in a small bowl and stir until smooth, then stir the paste into the cooking liquid. Switch the cooker to HIGH, re-cover and cook for 20 minutes until thickened.

Discard the fennel seed bundle and add a little more salt and pepper, if you like. Return the veal and vegetables to the cooker and heat through. Serve with polenta.

OSSO BUCCO

PREPARATION TIME: 25 minutes, plus making the stock (optional), gremolata, and risotto (optional)
COOKING TIME: 2½ hours on HIGH   **SERVES 4**

4 veal shank pieces, about 250g/9oz each, and 4cm/1½in thick

1 tbsp plain white flour

4 tbsp olive oil, plus extra if needed

1 carrot, finely diced

1 celery stick, finely chopped

1 onion, finely chopped

2 garlic cloves, finely chopped

4 tbsp dry red wine

2 tsp dried rosemary

250ml/9fl oz/1 cup Beef Stock (see page 168) or ready-made stock

250ml/9fl oz/1 cup passata

1 strip of lemon rind, pith removed

salt and freshly ground black pepper

1 recipe quantity Gremolata (see page 169), to serve

1 recipe quantity Saffron Risotto (see page 173), to serve (optional)

Season the veal shanks with salt and pepper, then dust with the flour, shaking off the excess. Heat 2 tablespoons of the oil in a large frying pan over a high heat. Reduce the heat to medium, add the veal shanks and fry for 5–8 minutes until browned on both sides, working in batches to avoid overcrowding the pan and adding extra oil, if necessary. Transfer the shanks to the slow cooker as they are brown.

Heat the remaining oil in the pan. Add the carrot, celery and onion and fry, stirring, for 2 minutes. Add the garlic and fry for a further 1–3 minutes until the onion is softened. Add the wine and rosemary and leave to bubble until the wine almost evaporates. Stir in the stock and passata and bring to the boil, scraping the bottom of the pan, and boil until the liquid has almost reduced by half. Add the lemon rind and season with salt and pepper. Pour over the veal shanks – they will not be completely covered with liquid.

Cover the cooker and cook on HIGH for 2½ hours until the meat is tender.

When the veal shanks are tender, remove and discard the lemon rind and add a little more salt and pepper, if you like. Spoon the cooking liquid over the veal shanks, sprinkle with Gremolata and serve with Saffron Risotto, if you like.

FISH & SHELLFISH

One of the unexpected discoveries of using a slow cooker is just how adept it is at cooking seafood. As you look through the diverse recipes in this chapter you'll find the selection includes both dishes that quietly simmer away, as well as quicker ones that are ready to eat in just over an hour, but still don't require much attention on your part. In either case, the gentle cooking of the slow cooker helps prevent the ultimate culinary disaster – overcooked seafood.

The transformation of hard, cardboard-like salt cod into tender, succulent fish has to be one of the miracles of the culinary world. To see how easily the slow cooker accomplishes this, try the Mediterranean Salt Cod recipe (see page 114).

For a retro dinner party starter that never fails to impress, try the delicious Salmon Terrine with Watercress Sauce (see page 116). It's ideal for entertaining because the terrine can be assembled in advance and be ready to cook just before your guests arrive. Then, as a bonus, if anyone is late, or you linger too long over drinks, you don't have to worry as the terrine will stay warm in the cooker.

◄ SALMON & SWEET POTATO CHOWDER (SEE PAGE 119)

MEDITERRANEAN SALT COD

PREPARATION TIME: 20 minutes, plus 24 hours soaking the cod and 30 minutes standing
COOKING TIME: 1 hour on HIGH plus 15 minutes on LOW   **SERVES 4**

400g/14oz dried salt cod fillet

4 garlic cloves, crushed

2 bay leaves, torn

2 fennel bulbs, quartered

1 onion, sliced

½ lemon, sliced

½ tbsp fennel seeds

4 tbsp extra virgin olive oil, plus extra to serve

3 tbsp milk

freshly ground black pepper

chopped parsley leaves, to serve

80g/2¾oz black olives, pitted and sliced, to serve

2 large chargrilled red peppers in oil, drained and sliced, to serve

slices of French bread, toasted, to serve

Put the cod in a non-metallic bowl. Cover with cold water and leave to soak for 24 hours, replacing the soaking water with fresh water 3 or 4 times.

One hour before the end of the soaking time, put the garlic, bay leaves, fennel, onion, lemon and fennel seeds in the slow cooker and pour over 750ml/26fl oz/3 cups boiling water.

Cover the cooker with the lid and cook on HIGH for 1 hour until the flavours are blended.

Drain the salt cod and rinse. Cut the cod into large pieces, if necessary. Add the rinsed cod to the cooker, flesh-side down. Switch the cooker to LOW, re-cover and cook for 15 minutes. Switch the cooker off and leave the cod to stand in the cooking liquid for a further 30 minutes, without lifting the lid.

Use a slotted spoon to remove the cod from the cooker and gently shake off any excess liquid. When the cod is cool enough to handle, wipe off the fennel seeds and flake the fish into large chunks, removing the skin and all small bones. Transfer three-quarters of the flesh to a food processor.

Heat the olive oil in a pan over a high heat until hot. Add 1 tablespoon of the hot olive oil to the food processor and process the cod. Continue adding the olive oil, 1 tablespoon at a time, until a thick purée forms. Add the milk and process again. Gently stir in the remaining flaked cod, and season with pepper. Sprinkle with parsley, olives and peppers and serve with slices of toast drizzled with olive oil.

SALMON TERRINE

PREPARATION TIME: 20 minutes, plus 15 minutes chilling, 10 minutes standing and making the sauce
COOKING TIME: 1½ hours on LOW   **SERVES 4**

400g/14oz boneless, skinless white fish, such as cod, haddock, monkfish, pollack and whiting, coarsely chopped with all pin bones removed

15g/½oz butter, plus extra for greasing

¼ tsp salt

1 egg white

150ml/5fl oz/scant ⅔ cup double cream

1 tbsp dried dill

finely grated zest of 1 lemon

200g/7oz boneless, skinless salmon fillets, about 5mm/¼in thick, cut into thin strips with all pin bones removed

salt and freshly ground black pepper

1 recipe quantity Watercress Sauce (see page 174)

Put an upturned heatproof saucer in the slow cooker. Grease a 500g/1lb 2oz loaf tin or other suitable dish that will fit on top of the saucer with the cooker lid in place. Line the base of the tin with greaseproof paper, then grease the base again.

Purée the white fish in a blender or food processor until smooth. With the motor still running, add the butter and salt and continue blending until incorporated. Add the egg white and incorporate. Transfer the fish paste to a bowl, then cover and chill for 15 minutes.

Slowly beat in the cream, 1 tablespoon at a time, until blended. Add the dill and lemon zest and season with salt and pepper. Spoon half of the mixture into the prepared tin and smooth the surface with a wet spatula. Arrange the salmon over the mixture. Very gently add the remaining white fish mixture and smooth the surface.

Cut out a piece of foil to cover the top of the tin with a 5mm/¼in overhang, then press it down over the edges of the tin. Put the tin on top of the saucer, then pour enough boiling water into the container to reach halfway up the sides of the tin.

Cover the cooker with the lid and cook on LOW for 1½ hours until the terrine is set and comes away from the tin. Switch the cooker off and leave the terrine to stand for 10 minutes. Remove the terrine from the cooker, then discard the foil and carefully pour out the cooking juices. Invert the terrine onto a plate and remove the tin and greaseproof paper. Cut into slices and serve with Watercress Sauce.

SALMON & SWEET POTATO CHOWDER

PREPARATION TIME: 20 minutes, plus making the stock (optional)
COOKING TIME: 4 hours 20 minutes on LOW   **SERVES 4**

15g/½oz butter

1 tbsp sunflower oil

1 celery stick, finely chopped

1 onion, finely chopped

4 tbsp plain white flour

125ml/4floz/½ cup Fish Stock (see page 168), weak Vegetable Stock (see page 169) or ready-made stock

750ml/26fl oz/3 cups milk

280g/10oz sweet potato, diced

2 bay leaves

1 long strip of lemon rind, pith removed

1 tbsp dried thyme

¼ tsp salt, plus extra to taste

700g/1lb 9oz boneless, skinless salmon fillets, about 2.5cm/1in thick, cut into bite-sized pieces

4 smoked streaky bacon rashers

freshly ground black pepper

finely chopped parsley leaves, to serve

smoked or sweet paprika, to serve

Heat the butter and oil in a large frying pan over a high heat. Reduce the heat to medium, add the celery and onion and fry, stirring, for 3–5 minutes until the onion is softened. Sprinkle over the flour and stir for 2 minutes to cook out the raw flavour. Pour over the stock and bring to the boil, stirring continuously to prevent lumps from forming. The mixture will be very thick and paste-like.

Slowly stir in the milk. Add the sweet potato, bay leaves, lemon rind, thyme and salt, then season with pepper. Cover and bring to the boil, then pour the mixture into the slow cooker.

Cover the cooker with the lid and cook on LOW for 4 hours until the sweet potato is tender. Gently stir in the salmon, re-cover and cook for a further 20 minutes until the salmon is cooked through and flakes easily.

Meanwhile, preheat the grill to high. When hot, grill the bacon for 2–3 minutes on each side until cooked and crisp. Drain well on kitchen paper, then chop very finely. Wrap in foil and keep warm.

When the salmon is cooked, remove and discard the bay leaves and lemon rind, and add a little more salt and pepper, if you like. Sprinkle with bacon, parsley and paprika and serve.

KEDGEREE

PREPARATION TIME: 20 minutes, plus making the stock (optional) and at least 5 minutes standing
COOKING TIME: 1 hour 15 minutes on HIGH   **SERVES 4**

2 tbsp sunflower oil

1 large onion, finely chopped

2 tbsp hot or mild curry paste, to taste

750ml/26fl oz/3 cups Vegetable Stock (see page 169) or ready-made stock

280g/10oz/1½ cups easy-cook white rice

¼ teaspoon salt, or to taste

4 eggs, at room temperature

2 undyed smoked haddock fillets, about 280g/10oz each, skinned and cut into bite-sized pieces

freshly ground black pepper

4 tbsp chopped coriander or parsley leaves, to serve

mango chutney, to serve (optional)

Heat the oil in a saucepan over a high heat. Reduce the heat to low, add the onion and fry, stirring frequently, for 8–10 minutes until golden brown. Stir in the curry paste and continue stirring for a further 1–2 minutes until fragrant.

Add the stock, increase the heat to high and bring to the boil, then pour the mixture into the slow cooker. Stir in the rice, add the salt and season with pepper. Gently push the eggs into the rice. The eggs will not be completely covered with liquid.

Cover the cooker with the lid and cook on HIGH for 1 hour. Gently stir the haddock into the rice. Turn the eggs over, quickly re-cover the cooker and cook for a further 15 minutes until the rice is tender and the haddock is cooked through and flakes easily. Remove the eggs from the cooker and leave to cool slightly.

Switch the cooker off. Put a clean kitchen towel over the kedgeree, re-cover with the lid and leave to stand for at least 5 minutes. The kedgeree can be left covered with the kitchen towel for up to 30 minutes. Add a little more salt and pepper, if you like.

Just before serving, and when cool enough to handle, shell and coarsely chop the eggs. Sprinkle the kedgeree with the chopped eggs and coriander, and serve with mango chutney, if you like.

CHIMICHURRI HADDOCK

PREPARATION TIME: 15 minutes, plus making the stock (optional)
COOKING TIME: 1 hour on HIGH, plus 12 minutes on LOW   **SERVES 4**

875ml/30fl oz/3½ cups Fish Stock (see page 168),
weak Vegetable Stock (see page 169) or
ready-made stock

2 bay leaves

1 fennel bulb, sliced

thinly pared rind of 1 lemon, pith removed

4 boneless, skinless haddock or cod fillets, about
150g/5½oz each and 2.5cm/1in thick

salt and freshly ground black pepper

lemon wedges, to serve

sautéed potatoes, to serve (optional)

CHIMICHURRI SAUCE

125ml/4fl oz/½ cup extra virgin olive oil, plus extra
if needed

2 tbsp lemon juice, plus extra to taste

2–4 large garlic cloves, finely chopped, to taste

1 red chilli, deseeded if you like, and finely sliced

2 tbsp finely chopped coriander leaves

2 tbsp chopped parsley leaves

salt and freshly ground black pepper

Put the stock, bay leaves, fennel and lemon rind in the slow cooker and season with salt and pepper.

Cover the cooker with the lid and cook on HIGH for 1 hour until the flavours are blended.

Switch the cooker to LOW. Add the haddock, re-cover and cook for 12 minutes until the haddock is cooked through and flakes easily. Use a fish slice to remove the fillets from the cooker, then pat dry with kitchen paper and transfer to plates.

Meanwhile, make the sauce. In a non-metallic bowl, whisk together the olive oil, lemon juice, garlic and chilli. Stir in the coriander and parsley and season with salt and pepper. Add a little more lemon juice, if you like. If not serving immediately, pour extra olive oil over the top of the sauce, cover and leave to one side until required.

Stir the sauce well and add a little more lemon juice or salt and pepper, if you like. Spoon 1 tablespoon of sauce over each fillet. Serve with lemon wedges, sautéed potatoes, if you like, and with the remaining sauce.

COOK'S TIP
Any leftover Chimichurri Sauce can be stored for up to 1 day, just pour extra olive oil over the top, cover and chill. It will lose its fresh colour but the flavour will intensify.

MEDITERRANEAN WHITE FISH STEW

PREPARATION TIME: 20 minutes, plus making the stock (optional) and aïoli
COOKING TIME: 1 hour on HIGH, plus 12 minutes on LOW   **SERVES 4**

2 tbsp olive oil

1 onion, sliced

1 leek, halved lengthways, sliced and rinsed

4 garlic cloves, finely chopped

4 tbsp aniseed-flavoured spirit or dry white wine

750ml/26fl oz/3 cups Fish Stock (see page 168), weak Vegetable Stock (see page 169) or ready-made stock

4 bay leaves

2 tsp dried dill

1 long strip of orange rind, pith removed

600g/1lb 5oz boneless, skinless mixed fish, such as hake, John Dory, monkfish, red mullet, sea bream and whiting, cut into bite-sized pieces

350g/12oz raw, peeled prawns, deveined

1 recipe quantity Aïoli (see page 169)

salt and freshly ground black pepper

chopped parsley leaves, to serve

slices of French bread, toasted, to serve

Heat the oil in a saucepan over a high heat. Reduce the heat to medium, add the onion and leek and fry, stirring, for 2 minutes. Add the garlic and fry for a further 1–3 minutes until the onion is softened.

Add the alcohol and boil for a few minutes until almost evaporated. Stir in the stock, bay leaves, dill and orange rind and season with salt and pepper. Pour the mixture into the slow cooker.

Cover the cooker with the lid and cook on HIGH for 1 hour until the flavours are blended. Switch the cooker to LOW, add the fish, then re-cover and cook until the fish is cooked through and flakes easily. Allow 12 minutes for pieces of fish 2.5cm/1in thick and 6 minutes for thin pieces of fish. Six minutes before the end of the cooking time, add the prawns and cook until they turn pink and curl. Use a slotted spoon to remove and discard any bones and the bay leaves. Transfer the fish and prawns to a bowl, cover with foil and keep warm.

Stir 2 tablespoons of the cooking liquid into the aïoli. Slowly whisk the aïoli into the cooking liquid, whisking continuously to prevent the sauce curdling. Add a little more salt and pepper, if you like. Return the fish and prawns to the cooker and heat through, if necessary. Sprinkle with parsley and serve with toast.

THAI FISH & COCONUT CURRY

PREPARATION TIME: 20 minutes, plus making the stock (optional)
COOKING TIME: 1 hour on HIGH, plus 12 minutes on LOW   **SERVES 4**

1 tbsp sunflower oil

2 shallots, thinly sliced

2 garlic cloves, crushed

1 Thai red chilli, deseeded if you like, and thinly sliced

1 tbsp shrimp paste

1 tsp turmeric

160ml/5¼fl oz/⅔ cup weak Vegetable Stock (see page 169) or ready-made stock

400ml/14fl oz/generous 1½ cups coconut milk

4 kaffir lime leaves

2.5cm/1in piece of galangal, peeled and sliced

2 tsp palm sugar or soft light brown sugar, plus extra to taste

juice of 1 lime, plus extra to taste

1 tsp fish sauce, or to taste (optional)

700g/1lb 9oz mixed boneless, skinless white fish, such as cod, hake, halibut or pollack, cut into large chunks

freshly ground black pepper

chopped coriander leaves, to serve

grated lime zest and lime halves, to serve

cooked basmati rice, to serve

bottled or tinned red chillies in vinegar, drained and sliced (optional), to serve

Preheat the covered slow cooker on HIGH. Heat the oil in a large frying pan over a high heat. Reduce the heat to medium, add the shallots and fry for 2 minutes. Add the garlic and chilli and fry for a further 1–3 minutes until the shallots are softened. Stir in the shrimp paste, then sprinkle over the turmeric.

Add the stock, coconut milk, lime leaves, galangal, palm sugar and lime juice and season with pepper. Bring to the boil, stirring to dissolve the shrimp paste and sugar, then pour the mixture into the slow cooker.

Cover the cooker with the lid and cook on HIGH for 1 hour until the flavours are blended. Add the fish sauce, if using, and add a little more sugar and lime juice, if you like.

Switch the cooker to LOW. Add the fish, re-cover and cook until the fish is cooked through and flakes easily. Allow 12 minutes for pieces of fish 2.5cm/1in thick and 6 minutes for thin pieces of fish.

Remove and discard the galangal. Sprinkle with coriander and lime zest and serve with lime halves, rice and sliced red chillies, if you like.

FISHERMAN'S SUPPER

Cooking squid either has to be lightning fast, or slow and gentle, making squid an ideal candidate for cooking in a slow cooker. With chorizo, saffron and chilli flakes, this recipe is inspired by numerous seafood stews along the Iberian coast.

PREPARATION TIME: 20 minutes, plus making the croûtes (optional)
COOKING TIME: 8 hours 20 minutes on LOW   **SERVES 4**

2 tbsp olive oil

150g/5½oz cooking chorizo, skinned and sliced

1 fennel bulb, thinly sliced with the fronds reserved

4 garlic cloves, crushed

a large pinch of saffron threads

a pinch of dried chilli flakes (optional)

125ml/4fl oz/½ cup dry white wine

800g/1lb 12oz/scant 3 cups tinned chopped tomatoes

12 new potatoes, scrubbed and halved or quartered if large, or 400g/14oz tinned chickpeas, drained and rinsed

200g/7oz fresh or defrosted, frozen squid rings

700g/1lb 9oz mixed fish, such as cod, hake, halibut, porgy or red mullet, on the bones and cut into large chunks

salt and freshly ground black pepper

1 recipe quantity Anchovy Croûtes (see page 171), to serve (optional)

Heat 1 tablespoon of the oil in a large frying pan over a high heat. Reduce the heat to medium, add the chorizo and fry, stirring, for 1–2 minutes until it gives off its fat and starts to crisp. Use a slotted spoon to transfer the chorizo to the slow cooker.

Heat the remaining oil in the pan. Add the fennel and fry, stirring, for 2 minutes. Add the garlic and fry for a further 1–3 minutes until the fennel is softened. Stir in the saffron and chilli flakes, if using.

Add the wine and boil until almost evaporated. Add the chopped tomatoes and potatoes and season with salt and pepper. Bring to the boil, stirring, and boil for 3 minutes. Pour the mixture into the cooker and stir in the squid rings.

Cover the cooker with the lid and cook on LOW for 8 hours until the squid rings and potatoes are tender. Use a large metal spoon to skim any excess fat from the surface of the cooking liquid, then stir.

Add the fish, re-cover and cook until the fish is cooked through and flakes easily. Allow 20 minutes for thick pieces of fish on the bone, 12 minutes for boneless fish 2.5cm/1in thick and 6 minutes for thin pieces of fish. Add a little more salt and pepper, if you like. Sprinkle with the reserved fennel fronds and serve with Anchovy Croûtes, if you like.

MOCK PAELLA

PREPARATION TIME: 15 minutes, plus making the stock (optional) and at least 5 minutes standing
COOKING TIME: 1 hour 15 minutes on HIGH   **SERVES 4**

1 tbsp olive oil

1 large onion, finely chopped

4 garlic cloves, finely chopped

250g/9oz cooking chorizo, skinned and diced

½ tsp smoked paprika

750ml/26fl oz/3 cups Chicken Stock (see page 168), Vegetable Stock (see page 169) or ready-made stock, plus extra if needed

500g/1lb 2oz fresh or defrosted, frozen mixed shellfish, such as mussels, prawns and squid rings

280g/10oz/1½ cups easy-cook white rice

2 red peppers, halved lengthways, deseeded and diced

a large pinch of saffron threads

½ teaspoon salt, or to taste

55g/2oz/⅓ cup frozen peas, defrosted

4 tbsp chopped parsley leaves

freshly ground black pepper

Heat the oil in a saucepan over a high heat. Reduce the heat to medium, add the onion and fry, stirring, for 2 minutes. Add the garlic and fry for a further 1–3 minutes until the onion is softened. Add the chorizo and paprika and stir for 1 minute, then use a spoon to remove any excess oil.

Add the stock, increase the heat to high and bring to the boil, then pour the mixture into the slow cooker. Stir in the shellfish, rice, peppers, saffron and salt, then season with pepper.

Cover the cooker with the lid and cook on HIGH for 1 hour. Stir in the peas, re-cover and cook for a further 15 minutes until the rice is tender and the peas are cooked through. Add a little more salt and pepper, if you like.

Switch the cooker off. Put a clean kitchen towel over the paella, re-cover with the lid and leave to stand for at least 5 minutes. The paella can be left covered with the kitchen towel for up to 30 minutes. Just before serving, stir in the parsley. Serve hot.

PRAWN & CRAB GUMBO

PREPARATION TIME: 50 minutes, plus making the stock (optional)
COOKING TIME: 1 hour 40 minutes on HIGH   **SERVES 4**

500g/1lb 2oz raw, large unpeeled prawns, peeled, heads removed and deveined, with heads and shells reserved

125ml/4fl oz/½ cup Fish Stock (see page 168) or ready-made stock

3 tbsp corn oil

100g/3½oz andouille sausage or cooking chorizo, skinned and sliced

55g/2oz/scant ½ cup plain white flour

1 large onion, chopped

4 garlic cloves, chopped

1 celery stick, halved lengthways and chopped

1 red pepper, halved lengthways, deseeded and diced

1 green pepper, halved lengthways, deseeded and diced

400g/14oz/scant 1⅔ cups tinned chopped tomatoes

85g/3oz green beans, chopped

4 okra, trimmed and sliced

2 bay leaves, torn

1 tbsp sweet paprika

1 tbsp dried dill

2 tsp dried thyme

½ tsp dried chilli flakes (optional)

225g/8oz fresh white crab meat

salt and freshly ground black pepper

finely chopped spring onions, to serve

cooked long-grain rice, to serve (optional)

hot pepper sauce, to serve

Put the reserved prawn shells and heads and the stock in a small saucepan and simmer, covered, over a medium-low heat until required.

Meanwhile, heat the oil in a frying pan over a high heat. Reduce the heat to low, add the sausage and fry, stirring, for 10 minutes until it gives off its fat. Use a slotted spoon to transfer the sausage to the slow cooker.

Sprinkle the flour into the remaining oil in the pan and stir to make a thick paste. Continue stirring for 15–20 minutes until the paste turns a hazelnut colour. It will be very slow to change colour, then change quickly, so watch closely so it does not burn.

Add the onion, garlic, celery and peppers and stir for a further 3–5 minutes until the onion is softened. Add the chopped tomatoes, green beans, okra, bay leaves, paprika, dill, thyme and chilli flakes, if using.

Strain the stock into the pan, discarding the solids, and bring to the boil, stirring. Season with salt and pepper, then pour the mixture into the cooker.

Cover the cooker with the lid and cook on HIGH for 1½ hours until the mixture has thickened. Stir in the prawns and crab meat, re-cover the cooker and cook for a further 10 minutes until the prawns turn pink and curl. Remove and discard the bay leaves and add a little more salt and pepper, if you like. Sprinkle with spring onions, and serve with rice, if you like, and with some hot pepper sauce.

VEGETARIAN

The recipes in this chapter highlight the exciting tastes of cuisines with a strong vegetarian culture. I particularly like vegetarian food from the Mediterranean and Far East – hearty casseroles and slowly simmered curries that are ideal for preparing in the slow cooker.

The Vegetable Tagine (see page 141) captures the spicy flavours of North Africa, while the Chickpea Curry (see page 138) and Lentil & Tomato Dahl (see page 142) are inspired by Indian cooking. The Thai-inspired Vegetable & Cashew Red Curry (see page 145) is a fragrant, warming recipe served up with naan bread. Claypot-Style Chinese Vegetables & Tofu (see page 146) is subtle and soothing at the end of a long day. It has become quite a favourite in my house.

Risottos are also one of my favourite foods but they are not naturally suited to being made in slow cookers. Pumpkin & Dolcelatte Rice (see page 132) has many similar characteristics, however, and the melting cheese added at the end of cooking provides the desired creaminess.

I hope this chapter provides inspiration for non-vegetarians, too. The recipes are packed with flavour and are very satisfying!

◄ RATATOUILLE (SEE PAGE 135)

PUMPKIN & DOLCELATTE RICE

This is as close as I think you can get to making an authentic risotto in a slow cooker.
It has all the flavour of an Italian classic.

PREPARATION TIME: 20 minutes, plus making the stock (optional)
COOKING TIME: 1½ hours on LOW   **SERVES 4**

1 tbsp olive oil, plus extra for greasing

150g/5½oz leeks, halved lengthways, thinly sliced and rinsed

2 large garlic cloves, chopped

100g/3½oz/½ cup arborio rice

1 tsp dried sage

4 tbsp dry white vermouth or dry white wine

500ml/17fl oz/2 cups Vegetable Stock (see page 169) or ready-made stock, plus extra if needed

¼ tsp salt, plus extra to taste

450g/1lb pumpkin, peeled, deseeded and chopped

85g/3oz dolcelatte cheese, rind removed and coarsely chopped

freshly ground black pepper

2 tbsp pumpkin seeds, toasted (see page 170), to serve

snipped chives, to serve

Grease the inside of the slow cooker container. Heat the oil in a large frying pan over a high heat. Reduce the heat to medium, add the leeks and fry, stirring, for 2 minutes. Add the garlic and fry for a further 1–3 minutes until the leeks have softened. Stir in the rice and sage.

Add the vermouth and boil until it evaporates. Add the stock and salt and season with pepper, then bring to the boil. Pour the mixture into the cooker and stir in the pumpkin.

Cover the cooker with the lid and cook on LOW for 1½ hours until the rice and pumpkin are tender.

When the rice and pumpkin are tender, add the dolcelatte and gently stir until it melts into the rice. Add a little more salt and pepper, if you like. Sprinkle with the toasted pumpkin seeds and chives and serve.

(4.30)

RATATOUILLE

Serve this ever-popular vegetable stew straight from the cooker or leave it to cool completely and enjoy with a selection of salads.

PREPARATION TIME: 20 minutes, plus making the stock (optional)
COOKING TIME: 4½ hours on HIGH   **SERVES 4**

5 tbsp olive oil or garlic-infused olive oil, plus extra to serve

350g/12oz aubergine, peeled and cubed

2 tbsp herbes de Provence or Italian dried mixed herbs

1 large onion, chopped

4 large garlic cloves, chopped

1 courgette, halved lengthways and thickly sliced

1 red pepper, halved lengthways, deseeded and sliced

400g/14oz tinned plum tomatoes

125ml/4fl oz/½ cup passata

2 tbsp Vegetable Stock (see page 169) or ready-made stock

1 tsp soft brown sugar

salt and freshly ground black pepper

basil leaves, to serve

French bread, to serve (optional)

Heat 2 tablespoons of the oil in a large frying pan over a high heat. Reduce the heat to medium, add half of the aubergine and fry, stirring, for 5–8 minutes until it absorbs the oil and begins to soften, then use a slotted spoon to transfer it to the slow cooker. Add another 2 tablespoons of the oil and repeat with the remaining aubergine. Sprinkle the herbs into the cooker.

Heat the remaining oil in the pan. Add the onion and fry, stirring, for 2 minutes. Add the garlic and fry for a further 1–3 minutes until the onion is softened.

Transfer the onion and garlic to the cooker. Add the courgette, pepper and plum tomatoes. Pour over the passata and stock, stir in the brown sugar and season with salt and pepper. The vegetables will not be completely covered with liquid.

Cover the cooker with the lid and cook on HIGH for 4½ hours, stirring once after 2 hours, until the vegetables are tender. Add a little more salt and pepper, if you like. Sprinkle with basil and serve hot or at room temperature with French bread drizzled with oil, if you like.

STUFFED PEPPERS

PREPARATION TIME: 20 minutes, plus making
the stock (optional)
COOKING TIME: 5 hours on LOW   **SERVES 4**

2 tbsp garlic-infused olive oil
1 red onion, finely chopped
40g/1½oz pine nuts, coarsely chopped
1 garlic clove, finely chopped
120g/4¼oz/½ cup easy-cook white or brown rice
250ml/9fl oz/1 cup Vegetable stock (see page 169)
    or ready-made stock, boiling
55g/2oz/heaped ⅓ cup currants or raisins
2 tbsp tomato purée
2 tbsp chopped parsley leaves
2 tbsp chopped mint leaves
½ tsp ground cinnamon
4 large red peppers, tops cut off and reserved, and
    deseeded, that will fit upright in the slow cooker
250ml/9fl oz/1 cup bottled tomato sauce, boiling
1 small handful of basil leaves, chopped
salt and freshly ground black pepper

Heat 1 tablespoon of the oil in a frying pan over a
medium heat. Add the onion and fry, stirring, for
2 minutes. Add the pine nuts and garlic and fry for
a further 1–3 minutes until the pine nuts are golden.

Transfer the mixture to a large bowl. Add the
rice, stock, currants, tomato purée, parsley, mint,
cinnamon and the remaining oil. Season with salt
and pepper. Divide the mixture into the peppers,
including all the liquid. Stand the peppers upright
in the cooker, using foil to support them, if necessary,
then top with the lids. Pour the tomato sauce into
the container and push the basil into the sauce.

Cover the cooker with the lid and cook on LOW for
5 hours until the rice is tender. Serve hot or chilled.

TABBOULEH TOMATOES

PREPARATION TIME: 20 minutes, plus making
the stock and frying the halloumi (optional)
COOKING TIME: 1½ hours on LOW   **SERVES 4**

4 large tomatoes, about 250g/9oz each, that will fit
    upright in the slow cooker
2 garlic cloves, peeled
185ml/6fl oz/¾ cup Vegetable Stock (see page 169)
    or ready-made stock, boiling
8 sun-dried tomatoes in oil, drained and finely chopped
115g/4oz/⅔ cup coarse bulgur wheat
4 tbsp chopped mint leaves, plus extra to serve
4 tbsp chopped parsley leaves
½ tsp ground allspice
a pinch of cayenne pepper, or to taste (optional)
salt and freshly ground black pepper
2 tbsp pine nuts, toasted (see page 170), to serve
1 recipe quantity Fried Halloumi (see page 172),
    to serve (optional)

Cut the top off each tomato and reserve. Scoop out
the pulp and seeds and discard. Sprinkle the insides
with salt, then turn upside-down to drain.

Put the garlic on a chopping board, sprinkle with
salt and use a knife to crush to a paste. Put the garlic
paste, stock, sun-dried tomatoes, bulgur wheat,
mint, parsley, allspice and cayenne pepper, if using,
in a bowl and stir. Season with salt and pepper.

Divide the mixture into the tomatoes, then top with
the lids. Stand the tomatoes upright in the slow
cooker, using foil to support them, if necessary.

Cover the cooker with the lid and cook on LOW for
1½ hours until the bulgur wheat is tender. Sprinkle
with toasted pine nuts and mint and serve hot or
cold with Fried Halloumi, if you like.

CHICKPEA CURRY

PREPARATION TIME: 15 minutes, plus making
the stock (optional)
COOKING TIME: 4 hours on LOW, plus 15 minutes
on HIGH **SERVES 4**

800g/1lb 12oz tinned chickpeas, drained and rinsed
4 large garlic cloves, finely chopped
4cm/1½in piece of root ginger, peeled and chopped
1 tbsp ghee, groundnut oil or sunflower oil
2 tsp cumin seeds
1 large onion, finely chopped
2 tbsp Madras curry powder
a pinch of dried chilli flakes, to taste (optional)
400g/14oz/scant 1⅔ cups tinned chopped tomatoes
55ml/1¾fl oz/¼ cup Vegetable Stock (see page 169)
   or ready-made stock
4 tbsp passata
200g/7oz baby spinach leaves, rinsed and shaken dry
salt and freshly ground black pepper
garam masala, to serve
warm naan breads, to serve

Put the chickpeas in the slow cooker. Put the garlic
and ginger in a mini food processor and process
until a coarse paste forms, then leave to one side.

Heat the ghee in a frying pan over a high heat.
Reduce the heat, add the cumin seeds and stir for
30 seconds. Add the onion and fry for 3–5 minutes.
Add the garlic paste, curry powder and chilli flakes,
if using, and fry for 30 seconds. Add the tomatoes,
stock and passata and bring to the boil, stirring, then
season. Pour the mixture into the cooker.

Cover the cooker with the lid and cook on LOW
for 4 hours. Switch the cooker to HIGH and stir in
the spinach. Cook, uncovered, for 10–15 minutes,
stirring once, until tender. Sprinkle with garam
masala and serve with naan breads.

TWO-BEAN CHILLI

PREPARATION TIME: 20 minutes, plus 8 hours
soaking the beans and making the tortilla chips
COOKING TIME: 1 hour on HIGH, plus 10 hours
on LOW **SERVES 4**

250g/9oz/scant 1¼ cups dried kidney beans, soaked
   in cold water for at least 8 hours
55g/2oz/heaped ¼ cup dried cannellini beans, soaked
   in cold water for at least 8 hours
4 garlic cloves, chopped
1 celery stick, chopped
1 onion, chopped
2 tbsp ancho chilli powder or chilli powder
1 tbsp dried thyme
1 tbsp dried mint
2 tsp ground coriander
2 tsp ground cumin
800g/1lb 12oz/scant 3 cups tinned chopped tomatoes
salt and freshly ground black pepper
chopped coriander leaves, to serve
soured cream, to serve
1 recipe quantity Tortilla Chips (see page 174), to serve

Bring a large, covered saucepan of unsalted
water to the boil. Drain all of the beans and
add them to the pan. Return to the boil and boil
vigorously for 10 minutes. Drain and rinse the
beans, then transfer them to the slow cooker.

Add all of the remaining ingredients, then pour
over 250ml/9fl oz/1 cup boiling water and stir,
adding a little extra water to cover the beans,
if necessary. Season with pepper.

Cover the cooker with the lid and cook on HIGH
for 1 hour. Switch the cooker to LOW and cook for
10 hours until the beans are tender. Season with salt
and a little pepper, if you like. Sprinkle with coriander
and serve with soured cream and Tortilla Chips.

BEANS & LENTILS WITH KALE

PREPARATION TIME: 25 minutes, plus at least 8 hours soaking the pulses,
and making the stock and croûtes (optional)
COOKING TIME: 6 hours 20 minutes on HIGH   **SERVES 4**

55g/2oz/scant ¼ cup dried mung beans, soaked in cold water for at least 8 hours

55g/2oz/¼ cup dried white beans, such as cannellini, soaked in cold water for at least 8 hours

2 tbsp split black lentils, soaked in cold water for at least 8 hours

2 tbsp green lentils, soaked in cold water for at least 8 hours

2 tbsp split red lentils, soaked in cold water for at least 8 hours

175g/6oz floury potatoes, such as Desiree, King Edward and Maris Piper, diced

8 garlic cloves, peeled

1 celery stick, thinly sliced

1 onion, grated

1 tbsp celery seeds

1 tbsp dried marjoram or dried oregano

500ml/17floz/2 cups Vegetable Stock (see page 169) or ready-made stock, boiling, plus extra if needed

250ml/9fl oz/1 cup passata

2 tsp soft light brown sugar

125g/4½oz green beans, chopped

100g/3½oz kale, rinsed and sliced

salt and freshly ground black pepper

chopped parsley leaves, to serve

1 recipe quantity Cheese & Mustard Croûtes (see page 171), to serve (optional)

Bring a large, covered saucepan of unsalted water to the boil. Drain all of the beans and lentils and add them to the pan. Re-cover the pan, return to the boil and boil vigorously for 10 minutes.

Meanwhile, put the potatoes, garlic, celery, onion, celery seeds and marjoram in the slow cooker.

At the end of the boiling time, drain and rinse the beans, then transfer to the cooker. Pour over the stock, adding extra to cover the beans and lentils, if necessary, and season with pepper.

Cover the cooker with the lid and cook on HIGH for 6 hours until all the beans and lentils are tender.

Add the passata, brown sugar, green beans and kale. Cook, uncovered, for a further 20 minutes until the green beans and kale are tender. Season with salt and a little more pepper, if you like. Sprinkle with parsley and serve with Cheese & Mustard Croûtes, if you like.

VEGETABLE TAGINE

PREPARATION TIME: 25 minutes, plus making the stock (optional)
COOKING TIME: 5 hours on LOW, plus 20 minutes on HIGH   **SERVES 4**

400g/14oz tinned chickpeas, drained and rinsed

150g/5½oz sweet potato, diced

100g/3½oz aubergine, peeled and diced

100g/3½oz carrot, diced

2 tbsp olive oil

1 large onion, finely chopped

4 garlic cloves, finely chopped

2 red peppers, halved lengthways, deseeded and chopped

2 tbsp harissa paste

½ tsp dried chilli flakes (optional)

400g/14oz/scant 1⅔ cups tinned chopped tomatoes

250ml/9fl oz/1 cup Vegetable Stock (see page 169) or ready-made stock

125ml/4fl oz/½ cup passata

60g/2¼oz/½ cup black olives, pitted

4 sun-dried tomatoes in oil, drained and finely chopped

1 preserved lemon, sliced

2 tbsp dried parsley

2 tbsp dried basil

½ tsp caster sugar

150g/5½oz courgette, diced

85g/3oz/⅔ cup sultanas or raisins

salt and freshly ground black pepper

coriander or mint sprigs, to serve

cooked couscous, to serve

Put the chickpeas, sweet potato, aubergine and carrot in the slow cooker.

Heat the oil in a large frying pan over a high heat. Reduce the heat to medium, add the onion and fry, stirring, for 2 minutes. Add the garlic and peppers and fry for a further 1–3 minutes until the onion is softened. Add the harissa paste and chilli flakes, if using, and stir for a further 30 seconds.

Add the chopped tomatoes, stock, passata, olives, sun-dried tomatoes, preserved lemon, parsley, basil and sugar and season with salt and pepper. Bring to the boil, stirring, then pour the mixture into the cooker and stir together. The vegetables will not be completely covered with liquid.

Cover the cooker with the lid and cook on LOW for 5 hours until the vegetables are tender.

Add the courgette and sultanas. Switch the cooker to HIGH and cook, uncovered, for 20 minutes until the courgette is tender. Remove and discard the preserved lemon slices and add a little more salt and pepper, if you like. Sprinkle with coriander and serve with couscous.

LENTIL DAHL

PREPARATION TIME: 15 minutes
COOKING TIME: 4 hours on HIGH   **SERVES 4**

150g/5½oz/heaped ⅔ cup split chana dal or dried yellow split peas, rinsed

100g/3½ oz/heaped ⅓ cup split red lentils, rinsed

1 onion, grated

4cm/1½in piece of root ginger

4 large garlic cloves, chopped

½ tsp turmeric

a large pinch of ground asafoetida

salt and freshly ground black pepper

garam masala, to serve

coriander leaves, to serve

warm naan breads, to serve (optional)

TEMPERING

55g/2oz ghee, or 2 tbsp groundnut oil or sunflower oil with 30g/1oz butter

2 dried red chillies, halved

2 tsp cumin seeds

1 tsp black mustard seeds

2 large tomatoes, deseeded and diced

Put the chana dal, lentils and onion in the slow cooker and pour over 800ml/28fl oz/scant 3½ cups boiling water.

Peel and coarsely chop half of the ginger. Put the chopped ginger and garlic in a mini food processor and process until a coarse paste forms, scraping down the side of the bowl as necessary. Add the paste to the cooker with the turmeric and asafoetida and season with pepper.

Cover the cooker with the lid and cook on HIGH for 4 hours until the lentils are tender.

Grate the remaining unpeeled ginger directly into the pot and season with salt and a little more pepper, if you like. Use a wooden spoon to stir and mash some of the lentils against the side of the container.

When the lentils are tender, make the tempering. Melt the ghee in a frying pan over a high heat. Add the chillies, cumin seeds and mustard seeds and stir for about 30 seconds until the seeds crackle. Add the tomatoes and continue stirring for 1–2 minutes until they soften. Watch closely so the seeds do not burn.

Ladle the dahl into bowls, then top with the tempering spices. Sprinkle with garam masala and coriander and serve with naan breads, if you like.

VEGETABLE & CASHEW RED CURRY

PREPARATION TIME: 20 minutes
COOKING TIME: 5 hours on LOW   **SERVES 4**

250g/9oz butternut squash, peeled, deseeded and diced

250g/9oz cauliflower, cut into small florets

3 tbsp groundnut oil or sunflower oil, plus extra if needed

1 red onion, finely chopped

4 garlic cloves, finely chopped

200g/7oz aubergine, cut into chunks

3 tbsp Thai red curry paste

400ml/14fl oz/generous 1½ cups coconut milk

100g/3½oz mangetout, trimmed

100g/3½oz/⅔ cup unsalted cashew nuts

2 kaffir lime leaves

juice of ½ lime, plus extra to taste

salt and freshly ground black pepper

1 red chilli, deseeded and thinly sliced, to serve

coriander leaves, to serve (optional)

2 tbsp pumpkin seeds, toasted (see page 170), to serve (optional)

warm naan breads, to serve

Put the squash and cauliflower in the slow cooker.

Heat 1 tablespoon of the oil in a large frying pan over a high heat. Reduce the heat to medium, add the red onion and fry, stirring, for 2 minutes. Add the garlic and fry for a further 1–3 minutes until the onion is softened. Use a slotted spoon to transfer the onion and garlic to the slow cooker.

Heat the remaining oil in the pan. Add the aubergine and fry, stirring, until softened. Add a little extra oil, if necessary. Stir in the curry paste and stir for 1 minute.

Add the coconut milk and bring to the boil, stirring, then pour the mixture into the cooker. Stir in the mangetout, cashew nuts, lime leaves and lime juice and season with salt and pepper.

Cover the cooker with the lid and cook on LOW for 5 hours until the squash and cauliflower are tender.

When the curry is cooked, stir well and add a little more lime juice, and salt and pepper, if you like. Sprinkle with red chilli, and with coriander and toasted pumpkin seeds, if you like. Serve with warm naan breads.

CLAYPOT-STYLE CHINESE VEGETABLES & TOFU

PREPARATION TIME: 25 minutes, plus making the stock (optional)
COOKING TIME: 1½ hours on LOW, plus 20 minutes on HIGH   **SERVES 4**

200g/7oz broccoli, cut into small florets

100g/3½oz cauliflower, cut into small florets

100g/3½oz baby sweetcorn, halved lengthways

100g/3½oz mangetout

1 carrot, thinly sliced

12 dried shiitake mushrooms, rinsed well

1 tbsp groundnut oil

1 onion, finely chopped

4 garlic cloves, chopped

1 tbsp Chinese five-spice powder

500ml/17fl oz/2 cups Vegetable Stock (see page 169) or ready-made stock

2 tbsp soy sauce, plus extra to taste

1 tbsp soft light brown sugar

4 cloves

1 cinnamon stick

1 star anise

a pinch of ground Szechuan pepper, plus extra to taste (optional)

200g/7oz Chinese cabbage, cored and finely shredded

200g/7oz/heaped 1 cup fried tofu, drained and cut into bite-sized pieces

freshly ground black pepper

toasted sesame oil, to serve

2 spring onions, finely shredded, to serve

Put the broccoli, cauliflower, baby sweetcorn, mangetout, carrot and shiitake mushrooms in the slow cooker.

Heat the oil in a frying pan over a high heat. Reduce the heat to medium, add the onion and fry, stirring, for 2 minutes. Add the garlic and fry for a further 1–3 minutes until the onion is softened. Add the Chinese five-spice powder and stir for 30 seconds.

Add the stock, soy sauce, brown sugar, cloves, cinnamon stick, star anise and Szechuan pepper, if using, and season with black pepper. Bring to the boil, stirring to dissolve the sugar, then pour the mixture into the cooker. The vegetables will not be completely covered with liquid.

Cover the cooker with the lid and cook on LOW for 1½ hours until the mushrooms are tender and the vegetables are tender but still retain a slight bite. Add the Chinese cabbage and add a little more soy sauce, Szechuan pepper and black pepper, if you like.

Switch the cooker to HIGH, re-cover and cook for 10 minutes. Add the tofu and cook for a further 10 minutes until the cabbage is tender.

Discard the cloves, cinnamon stick and star anise. Use a slotted spoon to divide the mushrooms, vegetables and tofu into bowls, then ladle over the broth. Drizzle with toasted sesame oil, sprinkle with spring onions and serve.

BUCKWHEAT, MUSHROOM & PEA CASSEROLE

PREPARATION TIME: 15 minutes, plus making the stock (optional) and 10 minutes standing
COOKING TIME: 1½ hours on LOW, plus 15 minutes on HIGH   **SERVES 4**

1 tbsp garlic-infused olive oil

2 onions, finely chopped

4 garlic cloves, finely chopped

1 tbsp dried rosemary

500g/1lb 2oz chestnut mushrooms, sliced

15g/½oz dried porcini mushrooms

100g/3½oz/heaped ½ cup buckwheat groats

200ml/7fl oz/generous ¾ cup Vegetable Stock (see page 169) or ready-made stock, plus extra if needed

4 tbsp tomato purée

1 tsp hot paprika, or to taste

a pinch of caster sugar

140g/5oz/scant 1 cup frozen peas, defrosted

2 tbsp chopped parsley leaves

2 tbsp snipped chives

salt and freshly ground black pepper

sunflower seeds, to serve

soured cream, to serve (optional)

Heat the oil in a large frying pan over a high heat. Reduce the heat to medium, add the onions and fry, stirring, for 2 minutes. Add the garlic and rosemary and fry for a further 1–3 minutes until the onions are softened. Add the chestnut mushrooms, sprinkle with salt and continue to fry until all the liquid is absorbed.

Put the porcini mushrooms in a sieve and rinse under cold running water to remove any dirt. Add the buckwheat, stock, tomato purée, paprika, sugar and the rinsed porcini mushrooms and stir until the tomato purée dissolves, then season with pepper. Transfer the ingredients to the slow cooker.

Cover the cooker with the lid and cook on LOW for 1½ hours until the buckwheat is tender. Stir in the peas, parsley and chives and add a little more salt and pepper, if you like. Switch the cooker to HIGH, re-cover and cook for 15 minutes until the peas are tender.

Switch off the cooker. Put a clean kitchen towel over the container, re-cover with the lid and leave to stand for 10 minutes for the steam to be absorbed. Just before serving, fluff up the buckwheat with a fork, then sprinkle with sunflower seeds and serve with soured cream, if you like.

DESSERTS

Don't overlook using your slow cooker when it comes to making desserts. The slow, gentle cooking technique makes slow cookers ideal for replacing a bain-marie in the oven, or a steamer on the hob, and for poaching fruit. Anybody who enjoys making desserts will enjoy the flexibility of using a slow cooker.

Egg-based desserts are conventionally cooked in a bain-marie to prevent the eggs curdling. You can create the same effect in your slow cooker, so, for example, you will end up with an Almond Crème Caramel (see page 159) or Pots de Crème au Chocolat (see page 157) with a satin-smooth texture. The slow cooker's low cooking temperature also make it ideal for desserts that are traditionally steamed on the hob, such as Spiced Bread Pudding (see page 165).

Date Pudding (see page 163) and Lemon Pudding (see page 164) are both great recipes for rounding off winter meals, but during warmer times of the year, try Summer Fruit with Polenta & Almond Topping (see page 156). I also enjoy the Winter Fruit Salad (see page 154) with a dollop of Greek yogurt for a breakfast on the run.

One word of caution with the recipes in this chapter: select a basin or dish that will fit in your slow cooker with the lid in place before you start cooking. You can improvise with whatever you have in your cupboard, as long as the volume remains the same.

◀ WINTER FRUIT SALAD (SEE PAGE 154)

SPICED FIGS

PREPARATION TIME: 15 minutes
COOKING TIME: 1¼ hours on HIGH
SERVES 4

150ml/5fl oz/scant ⅔ cup apple juice
110g/3¾oz/heaped ½ cup soft light brown sugar
1 tbsp clear honey
1 cinnamon stick
a pinch of ground cloves
1 vanilla pod, split lengthways, or ½ tsp vanilla extract
24 dried figs
1 tsp lemon juice (optional)
vanilla ice cream or crème fraîche, to serve

Put the apple juice, brown sugar and honey in the slow cooker. Stir until the sugar and honey dissolve, then add the cinnamon stick, cloves and vanilla pod.

Cover the cooker with the lid and cook on HIGH for 45 minutes. Add the figs, re-cover and cook for a further 30 minutes until they are soft but holding their shape. Serve the figs hot with scoops of ice cream.

Alternatively, serve the figs with a thicker syrup. Use a slotted spoon to transfer the figs to a bowl, then leave to one side. Pour the syrup and spices into a small saucepan and boil over a high heat for 8 minutes, or until reduced. If the syrup is too sweet, stir in the lemon juice. Pour over the figs and serve with scoops of ice cream.

If not serving immediately, leave the figs to cool completely, then cover and chill until required. The figs can be kept in the fridge for up to 1 week.

CHERRY & KIRSCH COMPOTE

PREPARATION TIME: 20 minutes, plus cooling
COOKING TIME: 1½ hours on HIGH   **SERVES 4**

200g/7oz/scant 1 cup caster sugar
1 vanilla pod, split lengthways, or ½ tsp vanilla extract
900g/2lb cherries, stems removed
2 tbsp blanched almonds
1 tbsp kirsch
2 tbsp flaked almonds, toasted (see page 170),
   to decorate
vanilla or chocolate ice cream, to serve (optional)

Preheat the covered slow cooker on HIGH while you assemble the ingredients.

Put the sugar in the cooker and pour over 125ml/4fl oz/½ cup boiling water. Stir until the sugar dissolves, then add the vanilla pod.

Cover the cooker with the lid and cook on HIGH for 45 minutes. Add the cherries and blanched almonds, then re-cover the cooker and cook for a further 45 minutes until the cherries are tender.

Strain into a bowl, reserving the syrup, and leave the cherries and syrup to cool. When the cherries are cool, remove the vanilla pod and the blanched almonds. When the syrup is cool, stir in the cherries and kirsch.

Sprinkle with toasted almonds and serve with scoops of ice cream, if you like. If not serving immediately, cover and chill until required. The compote can be kept in the fridge for up to 3 days.

VANILLA & PEPPER-POACHED PEARS

PREPARATION TIME: 15 minutes, plus cooling, at least 2 hours chilling, and making the sauce (optional)
COOKING TIME: 1 hour 50 minutes on HIGH   **SERVES 4**

375ml/13fl oz/1½ cups sweet white wine or orange juice

100g/3½oz/scant ½ cup caster sugar

1 vanilla pod, split lengthways

1 tbsp black peppercorns, lightly crushed

thinly pared rind of 1 large orange, pith removed, plus extra finely grated orange zest, to decorate

4 pears, such as Conference, about 200g/7oz each

1 recipe quantity Hot Chocolate Sauce (see page 175), to serve (optional)

Preheat the covered slow cooker on HIGH while you assemble the ingredients.

Put the wine, sugar, vanilla pod, peppercorns and orange rind in the cooker, and stir until the sugar dissolves.

Cover the cooker with the lid and cook on HIGH for 1½ hours.

Fifteen minutes before the end of the cooking time, peel the pears, leaving the stalks intact. Use an apple corer or small metal spoon to remove the cores from the bottom of each pear, then level the bases with a knife so the pears will stand upright.

Put the pears in the cooker and spoon the wine mixture over them. The pears will only be half submerged in the liquid. Re-cover the cooker and cook for a further 20 minutes until the pears are tender but holding their shape. Use a slotted spoon to remove the pears from the cooker, then transfer them to a bowl and leave to cool completely.

Transfer the cooking juices to a small saucepan and boil until reduced by two-thirds. Strain the syrup into a bowl and discard the orange rind and peppercorns. Leave the syrup to cool completely.

Once cooled, spoon the syrup over the pears. Cover and chill for at least 2 hours and up to 48 hours. Sprinkle the pears and syrup with orange zest and serve with Hot Chocolate Sauce, if you like.

COOK'S TIP
The vanilla pods can be wiped, dried and used again.

WINTER FRUIT SALAD

It's best to use firm dried fruit for this, rather than the plumped 'ready-to-eat' varieties. If, however, you only have the softer fruit in your cupboard, reduce the cooking time in the second step to 1 hour before you add the smaller fruit.

PREPARATION TIME: 15 minutes, plus 30 minutes steeping
COOKING TIME: 2½ hours on HIGH   **SERVES 4**

450g/1lb dried fruit, such as apples, apricots, mangoes or prunes

250ml/9fl oz/1 cup orange juice, plus extra if needed

8 green cardamom pods, lightly crushed

6 Earl Grey tea bags

1 cinnamon stick

thinly pared rind of 1 lemon, pith removed

thinly pared rind of 1 orange, pith removed

55g/2oz/scant ⅓ cup soft light brown sugar, plus extra if needed

2 tbsp dried cranberries

2 tbsp currants

2 tbsp sultanas

2 tbsp hazelnuts (optional)

lemon juice, to taste (optional)

Greek yogurt, to serve

Put the dried fruit, orange juice, cardamom pods, tea bags, cinnamon stick and lemon and orange rinds in the slow cooker – do not turn the cooker on. Pour over 750ml/26fl oz/3 cups boiling water, then cover with the lid and leave to steep for 30 minutes.

Switch the cooker to HIGH. Remove and discard the tea bags. Add the brown sugar and stir until it dissolves. Re-cover the cooker and cook for 1½ hours. Stir in the cranberries, currants and sultanas, re-cover and cook for a further 1 hour until all the fruit is soft and the flavours are blended.

Meanwhile, toast the hazelnuts, if using. Heat a frying pan over a medium heat, add the hazelnuts and dry-fry for 3–4 minutes until lightly browned, shaking the pan occasionally to ensure they do not burn. Leave to cool slightly, then rub off the skins, chop and leave to one side.

When the fruit salad is cooked, taste and add lemon juice, if you like, or a little more orange juice or brown sugar, depending on how tart the fruit is. Sprinkle with the toasted hazelnuts, if using, and serve hot with dollops of yogurt. If not serving immediately, leave the salad to cool completely, then cover and chill until required. Leftovers can be kept refrigerated in an airtight container for up to 1 week.

SUMMER FRUIT WITH POLENTA & ALMOND TOPPING

PREPARATION TIME: 20 minutes, plus 5 minutes standing
COOKING TIME: 4½ hours on HIGH   **SERVES 4**

400g/14oz mixed summer berries, such as blackberries and raspberries

3 baking apples, such as Granny Smiths, peeled, cored and chopped

2 tbsp soft light brown sugar, plus extra if needed

2 tsp arrowroot or cornflour

finely grated zest of 1 orange

icing sugar, to decorate

vanilla ice cream, to serve (optional)

POLENTA & ALMOND TOPPING

75g/2½oz butter, softened

75g/2½oz/⅓ cup caster sugar

1 large egg plus 1 extra large yolk, beaten together

¾ tsp almond extract

75g/2½oz/½ cup medium polenta

60g/2¼oz/½ cup white self-raising white flour

¾ tsp baking powder

2 tbsp flaked almonds

Select a 15cm/6in soufflé dish or 750ml/26fl oz/ 3-cup heatproof dish that will fit in the slow cooker with the lid in place and leave to one side. Line the base of the container with foil, then preheat the covered cooker on HIGH.

Put the berries and apples in a saucepan. Sprinkle over the brown sugar and arrowroot and toss lightly to coat the fruit. Put the pan over a high heat and stir gently until the sugar dissolves and the juices start to run. Stir in the orange zest and add a little more sugar, if you like, depending on how tart the fruit is. Turn off the heat, cover and leave to stand while you make the topping.

To make the topping, put the butter and sugar in a large bowl and beat until light and fluffy. Beat in the eggs and almond extract, then beat in the polenta. Sift the flour and baking powder into the bowl and fold in, using a metal spoon.

Return the fruit to a high heat and bring to the boil. Pour the fruit and juices into the dish, then immediately spoon the topping in 4–6 mounds over the top – the topping will be too stiff to spread but it will meld together as it cooks. Sprinkle the almonds over the top and put the dish in the cooker.

Cover the cooker with the lid and cook on HIGH for 4½ hours until the topping is set.

Remove the dish and leave to stand for 5 minutes. Sift over some icing sugar and serve with scoops of ice cream, if you like.

POTS DE CRÈME AU CHOCOLAT

PREPARATION TIME: 15 minutes, plus cooling and at least 4 hours chilling
COOKING TIME: 1 hour on LOW   **SERVES 4**

5 large egg yolks

500ml/17fl oz/2 cups double cream, plus 60ml/2fl oz/¼ cup to serve

2 tbsp caster sugar, plus 4 tbsp to serve

¼ tsp vanilla extract

a pinch of salt

115g/4oz dark chocolate, 70% cocoa solids, chopped, plus 15g/½oz to serve

Select four 150ml/5fl oz/scant ⅔-cup heatproof pots that will fit in the slow cooker with the lid in place and leave to one side.

Beat the egg yolks in a large heatproof bowl. Put the cream, sugar, vanilla extract and salt in a small saucepan over a medium heat and stir until the sugar dissolves. Increase the heat to high and bring to the boil. Add the chocolate and stir until it melts.

Add the chocolate mixture to the egg yolks, whisking continuously, until blended. Strain the mixture into a jug, then pour into the pots. Cover the top of each pot with cling film, then put them in the cooker. Pour enough boiling water into the container to reach halfway up the sides of the pots.

Cover the cooker with the lid and cook on LOW for 1 hour until the custards are set around the edge but slightly wobbly in the centres. Carefully lift the chocolate pots out of the cooker, then remove the cling film and leave to cool completely. Re-cover with cling film and chill for at least 4 hours and up to 24 hours. The custards will firm up as they chill.

Just before serving, whip the 60ml/2fl oz/¼ cup cream until soft peaks form. Sprinkle over the 4 tablespoons of sugar and whip until stiff. Add a spoonful of cream to the top of each pot, then grate over the dark chocolate and serve.

ALMOND CRÈME CARAMEL

PREPARATION TIME: 15 minutes, plus cooling and at least 12 hours chilling
COOKING TIME: 1½ hours on LOW   **SERVES 4**

125g/4½oz/heaped ½ cup caster sugar, plus
1 tbsp extra

a drop of lemon juice

600ml/21fl oz/scant 2½ cups milk

4 eggs

¼ tsp almond extract

2 tbsp flaked almonds, toasted (see page 170),
to serve

Put an upturned heatproof saucer in the slow cooker.

Put the sugar and 125ml/4fl oz/½ cup water in a small, stainless steel saucepan over a medium heat and stir until the sugar dissolves. Increase the heat to high and boil for 3–5 minutes without stirring, until the caramel turns a dark golden brown. Watch closely because it can burn quickly. Immediately remove the pan from the heat and add the lemon juice to stop the cooking process. Pour the caramel into a 15cm/6in soufflé dish and leave to one side.

Put the milk in a saucepan and heat over a high heat until it just reaches boiling point, then remove from the heat. Put the eggs, almond extract and extra sugar in a bowl and beat until the sugar dissolves. Add the milk and mix together, beating constantly. Strain the mixture over the caramel and cover with cling film. Put the dish on top of the saucer in the cooker. Pour enough boiling water into the container to reach halfway up the side of the dish.

Cover the cooker with the lid and cook on LOW for 1½ hours until the custard is set and a knife inserted in the centre comes out clean. Remove the crème caramel from the cooker, uncover and leave to cool completely, then cover and chill for at least 12 hours.

Just before serving, run a knife around the edge of the dish. Place a rimmed serving dish upside-down over the top of the soufflé dish, hold the two firmly together, invert and shake. Carefully remove the dish. Sprinkle the crème caramel with toasted almonds and serve. This is best made at least 1 day before serving; it will keep in the refrigerator for up to 3 days.

CREAMY RICE PUDDING

PREPARATION TIME: 10 minutes
COOKING TIME: 1½ hours on HIGH   **SERVES 4**

butter, softened, for greasing

3 tbsp caster sugar

2 tbsp cornflour

685ml/23½fl oz/2¾ cups milk

100g/3½oz/scant ½ cup pudding rice or other short-grain rice

a pinch of salt

finely grated zest of 1 lemon, plus extra to decorate

2 tsp lemon juice, or to taste (optional)

2 tbsp chopped pistachio nuts, to serve

freshly grated nutmeg, to serve

125ml/4fl oz/½ cup double cream, to serve, if needed

Grease the bottom and sides of the slow cooker container. Preheat the covered cooker on HIGH while you assemble the ingredients.

Put the sugar and cornflour in the cooker. Slowly whisk in the milk, and continue whisking until the sugar and cornflour dissolve – make sure there are not any lumps. Stir in the rice and salt.

Cover the cooker with the lid and cook on HIGH for 15 minutes. Stir well, making sure to incorporate any cornflour that has sunk to the bottom of the container. Re-cover the cooker and cook for a further 15 minutes, then stir again.

Stir in the lemon zest, re-cover and cook for a further 1 hour, without stirring, until the rice is tender and the pudding is thick and creamy. Slowly stir in a little lemon juice, if using. Sprinkle with extra lemon zest, pistachios and nutmeg and serve hot.

If not serving immediately, transfer the rice pudding to a bowl and leave to cool completely, then cover and chill for up to 24 hours. The pudding will have thickened quite a bit, so stir in the cream, if necessary, and serve chilled with lemon zest, pistachios and nutmeg.

DATE PUDDING

PREPARATION TIME: 20 minutes, plus making the sauce
COOKING TIME: 1½ hours on HIGH   **SERVES 4**

100g/3½oz/heaped ½ cup pitted dates, chopped

½ tsp bicarbonate of soda

75g/2½oz butter, softened, plus extra for greasing

100g/3½oz/scant ½ cup caster sugar

1 egg, beaten

½ tsp vanilla extract

125g/4½oz/1 cup self-raising white flour

a pinch of salt

1 recipe quantity Dark Toffee Sauce (see page 175), to serve

vanilla ice cream, to serve (optional)

Put an upturned heatproof saucer in the slow cooker. Grease a 15cm/6in soufflé dish or 750ml/26fl oz/3-cup heatproof dish that will fit on top of the saucer with the cooker lid in place. Cut out a circle of foil to cover the top of the dish with a 2.5cm/1in overhang and leave to one side.

Put the dates, bicarbonate of soda and 200ml/7fl oz/scant 1 cup water in a saucepan over a medium heat and simmer, stirring occasionally, for 5 minutes, until the dates are softened. Remove the pan from the heat and leave to cool slightly.

Put the butter and sugar in a large bowl and beat until light and fluffy, then beat in the egg and the vanilla extract. Sift the flour and salt into the bowl and beat it in. Add the dates and their soaking liquid and fold in.

Spoon the mixture into the prepared dish and smooth the surface. Cover the dish with cling film, then with the foil, and tie a piece of string tightly around the rim of the dish to secure it. Put the dish on top of the saucer, then pour enough boiling water into the container to reach halfway up the side of the dish.

Cover the cooker with the lid and cook on HIGH for 1½ hours until the pudding is firm to the touch and a skewer inserted in the centre comes out clean.

Remove the date pudding from the cooker. Carefully remove the foil and cling film and leave to stand in the dish for 2 minutes. Serve with hot Dark Toffee Sauce and scoops of ice cream, if you like.

LEMON PUDDING

PREPARATION TIME: 20 minutes, plus 5 minutes standing, and making the sauce (optional)
COOKING TIME: 8 hours on HIGH   **SERVES 4**

115g/4oz butter, softened, plus extra for greasing

115g/4oz/½ cup caster sugar

2 eggs

½ tsp vanilla extract

175g/6oz/scant 1½ cups self-raising white flour

a pinch of salt

3 tbsp finely grated lemon zest, or a mixture of lemon, lime and orange zests

3–4 tbsp lemon juice

1 recipe quantity Butterscotch Sauce (see page 175), to serve (optional)

Put an upturned heatproof saucer in the slow cooker. Grease a 1l/35fl oz/4-cup pudding basin or heatproof bowl that will fit on top of the saucer with the cooker lid in place. Line the base of the basin with greaseproof paper, then grease the base again. Cut out a circle of foil to cover the top of the basin with a 5cm/2in overhang and set aside.

Put the butter and sugar in a large bowl and beat until light and fluffy, then beat in the eggs, one at a time, and the vanilla extract. Sift in the flour and salt, add the lemon zest and fold in. Gradually stir in the lemon juice until the mixture is a soft dropping consistency.

Spoon the mixture into the prepared basin and smooth the surface. Cover the basin with cling film, then with the foil, and tie a piece of string tightly around the rim of the basin to secure it. Put the basin on top of the saucer, then pour enough boiling water into the container to reach halfway up the side of the basin.

Cover the cooker with the lid and cook on HIGH for 8 hours until the pudding is well risen and a skewer inserted in the centre comes out clean. Remove the lemon pudding from the cooker. Carefully remove the foil and cling film and leave the pudding to stand in the basin for 5 minutes.

Run a knife around the edge of the basin. Place a rimmed serving dish upside-down over the basin, hold the two firmly together, invert, giving a firm shake halfway over. Remove the basin, peel off the greaseproof paper and serve with hot Butterscotch Sauce, if you like.

SPICED BREAD PUDDING

PREPARATION TIME: 15 minutes, plus 22 minutes standing, and making the sauce (optional)
COOKING TIME: 5 hours on HIGH   **SERVES 4**

55g/2oz butter, plus extra for greasing

200ml/7fl oz/¾ cup + 2 tbsp milk

2 tsp ground mixed spice

finely grated zest of 1 orange

a pinch of salt

280g/10oz day-old white bread, torn into small pieces

175g/6oz/scant 1 cup soft light brown sugar, plus 2 tbsp extra

225g/8oz/1¼ cups mixed ready-to-eat dried fruit, such as apricots, cranberries, currants, raisins and sultanas, chopped, if necessary

½ tsp almond extract

2 eggs, beaten

1 recipe quantity Fresh Orange Sauce (see page 175), to serve (optional)

Grease a 450g/1lb loaf tin or 750ml/26fl oz/3-cup heatproof dish that will fit in the slow cooker with the lid in place and leave to one side. Preheat the covered cooker on HIGH, while you assemble the ingredients.

Put the butter, 150ml/5fl oz/scant ⅔ cup of the milk, the mixed spice, orange zest and salt in a large saucepan over a medium heat and bring to a simmer. Add the bread, brown sugar, dried fruit and almond extract, and stir until the bread softens. Remove the pan from the heat and leave to stand for 20 minutes.

Beat in the eggs, then add enough of the remaining milk to form a soft and moist, but not mushy, mixture. Spoon the mixture into the prepared tin and sprinkle the extra brown sugar over the top. Cover the tin with cling film and put it in the cooker.

Cover the cooker with the lid and cook on HIGH for 5 hours until the pudding is set.

Remove the bread pudding from the cooker and leave to stand in the tin for 2 minutes. Remove the cling film and run a knife around the edges of the tin. Place a chopping board over the pudding, hold the two firmly together, invert, giving a firm shake halfway over, and remove the tin. Slice the pudding and serve with hot Fresh Orange Sauce, if you like.

COOK'S TIP
Any leftover bread pudding can be eaten at room temperature, making it ideal for including in lunchboxes.

TRADITIONAL CHRISTMAS PUDDING

A slow cooker really comes into its own at Christmas. Use it to make or reheat the pudding, freeing up hob space. To reheat, cover with cling film and foil as below, add to the cooker on an upturned saucer and pour enough boiling water into the container to come halfway up the side of the basin. Cover and reheat on HIGH for 3 hours.

PREPARATION TIME: 25 minutes, plus 45 minutes standing and making the butter
COOKING TIME: 6 hours on HIGH   **SERVES 4**

155g/5½oz/1¼ cups raisins

110g/3¾oz/¾ cup currants

55g/2oz/scant ½ cup sultanas

6 tbsp brandy or orange juice

1 cooking apple, about 180g/6¼oz, peeled, cored and grated

2 large eggs, beaten

150g/5½oz grated suet

125g/4½oz/1¼ cups fresh breadcrumbs

55g/2oz/scant ½ cup self-raising white flour

30g/1oz/⅓ cup ground almonds

75g/2½oz/⅓ cup firmly packed soft dark brown sugar

2 tbsp chopped candied lemon peel

2 tbsp chopped candied orange peel

1 tbsp ground mixed spice

1 tsp ground cloves

½ tsp ground nutmeg

a pinch of salt

butter, for greasing

1 recipe quantity Brandy Butter (see page 175), to serve

Put the raisins, currants, sultanas and brandy in a bowl. Leave to stand for 30 minutes. Add all the remaining ingredients and stir.

Meanwhile, put an upturned heatproof saucer in the slow cooker. Grease a 1l/35fl oz/4-cup pudding basin or heatproof bowl that will fit on top of the saucer with the cooker lid in place. Line the base of the basin with greaseproof paper, then grease the base again. Cut out a circle of foil to cover the top of the basin with a 2.5cm/1in overhang and set aside.

Spoon the fruit mixture into the basin and smooth the surface. The mixture will be about 2.5cm/1in below the rim. Cover the basin with cling film, then with the foil and tie a piece of string tightly around the basin rim to secure it. Put the basin on top of the saucer, then pour enough boiling water into the container to reach halfway up the side of the basin.

Cover the cooker with the lid and cook on HIGH for 6 hours until set. Remove the pudding from the cooker. Carefully remove the foil and cling film and leave to stand in the basin for 15 minutes. Place a serving plate upside-down over the pudding, hold the two firmly together, invert, giving a firm shake halfway over, and remove the basin. Peel off the greaseproof paper. Serve hot with Brandy Butter.

BASIC RECIPES & ACCOMPANIMENTS

STOCKS

BEEF STOCK

Don't be tempted to skip the first step. It is this slow browning that gives the stock its dark brown colour and depth of flavour.

PREPARATION TIME: 50 minutes
COOKING TIME: 10 hours on LOW
MAKES ABOUT 1.1l/38fl oz/4½ cups

500g/1lb 2oz beef bones, chopped
500g/1lb 2oz boneless beef shin, trimmed and
    cut into large chunks
1 carrot, sliced
1 celery stick, sliced
1 onion, sliced
2 bay leaves, tied together with several parsley sprigs and
    thyme sprigs
1 tsp black peppercorns

Preheat the oven to 220°C/425°F/Gas 7. Put the beef bones, beef shin, carrot, celery and onion in a roasting tin and roast for 40 minutes, stirring often.

Transfer the beef, bones and vegetables to the slow cooker. Add the herb bundle and peppercorns and pour over 1.25l/44fl oz/5 cups water.

Cover the cooker and cook on LOW for 10 hours. Use a large metal spoon to skim any excess fat from the surface of the cooking liquid, then strain the stock into a large bowl, discarding the solids.

If not using immediately, leave to cool completely, then cover and chill. Once chilled, remove any fat from the surface. Keep refrigerated and use within 2 days or freeze for up to 3 months.

CHICKEN STOCK

If I'm not in the mood or don't have time to make stock after I've roasted a chicken, I simply put the bones in the freezer until I want them. If you do this, be sure to defrost the bones and let them come to room temperature before adding to the slow cooker.

PREPARATION TIME: 10 minutes
COOKING TIME: 10 hours on LOW
MAKES ABOUT 1.4l/48fl oz/5½ cups

1 large carrot, sliced
1 celery stick, chopped
1 onion, sliced
2 tsp black peppercorns, lightly crushed
2 tbsp dried mixed herbs or dried parsley
680g/1lb 8oz cooked chicken carcass or bones, chopped
    to fit in the slow cooker
salt

Put the carrot, celery, onion, peppercorns, mixed herbs and chicken in the slow cooker and pour over 1.5l/52fl oz/6 cups water.

Cover the cooker and cook on LOW for 10 hours. Strain the stock into a large bowl, discarding the solids.

If not using immediately, leave to cool completely, then cover and chill. Once chilled, remove any fat from the surface. Keep refrigerated and use within 2 days or freeze for up to 3 months.

FISH STOCK

PREPARATION TIME: 10 minutes
COOKING TIME: 2 hours on LOW
MAKES ABOUT 1.5l/52fl oz/6 cups

1 onion, sliced
1 bay leaf, tied together with several parsley sprigs and a
    piece of leek
1 tsp black peppercorns, lightly crushed
700g/1lb 9oz white fish heads, bones and trimmings

Put the onion, herb bundle and peppercorns in the slow cooker, then top with the fish heads, bones and trimmings. Pour over 1.65l/56fl oz/scant 6½ cups water.

Cover the cooker and cook on LOW for 45 minutes. Use a large metal spoon to skim any foam from the surface of the cooking liquid. Re-cover the cooker and cook for a further 1¼ hours. Strain the stock into a large bowl, discarding the solids.

If not using immediately, leave to cool completely, then cover and chill. Keep refrigerated and use within 1 day or freeze for up to 3 months.

VEGETABLE STOCK

PREPARATION TIME: 10 minutes
COOKING TIME: 8 hours on LOW
MAKES ABOUT 1.4l/48fl oz/5½ cups

4 celery sticks, chopped, with the tops reserved
1 carrot, sliced
1 leek, sliced and rinsed
1 onion, sliced, with the skin reserved, if you like
2 bay leaves, tied together with several parsley sprigs and
   thyme sprigs
1 tsp black peppercorns, lightly crushed

Put the celery, carrot, leek, onion, herb bundle, peppercorns and the onion skin, if using, in the slow cooker – the onion skin will give the stock a dark golden colour. Pour over 1.5l/52fl oz/6 cups water, adding extra to cover all of the vegetables, if necessary.

Cover the cooker and cook on LOW for 8 hours. Strain the stock into a large bowl, discarding the solids.

If not using immediately, leave to cool completely, then cover and chill. Keep refrigerated and use within 2 days or freeze for up to 3 months.

OTHER BASIC RECIPES

AÏOLI

PREPARATION TIME: 15 minutes
MAKES enough for 1 fish stew

2 egg yolks
8 garlic cloves, roughly chopped
310ml/10¾fl oz/1¼ cups extra virgin olive oil

1 tsp lemon juice, plus extra to taste
salt and freshly ground black pepper

Put the egg yolks and garlic in a mini food processor and process until the garlic is puréed. With the motor running, slowly add the oil, drop by drop, and continue to process until incorporated. As the sauce begins to thicken add the oil in a steady stream until thickened and smooth.

Add 1 teaspoon warm water and the lemon juice and season with salt and pepper. Blend again and add a little more lemon juice and salt and pepper, if you like.

If not using immediately, transfer the aïoli to a bowl and cover. Keep refrigerated for up to 1 day before using.

CHEESE & HERB DUMPLINGS

PREPARATION TIME: 10 minutes
SERVES 4

75g/2½oz/¾ cup dried breadcrumbs
75g/2½oz/heaped ½ cup self-raising white flour
55g/2oz cold butter, diced
60g/2¼oz/½ cup coarsely grated full-flavoured cheese,
   such as Cheddar or Parmesan
1 tbsp finely snipped chives
1 tbsp finely chopped parsley leaves

Put the breadcrumbs, flour and butter in a blender or food processor and blend until the mixture resembles coarse breadcrumbs. Transfer to a bowl, then add the cheese and herbs and combine the ingredients. Wet your hands, divide the mixture into 8 equal portions and roll into balls.

If not using immediately, cover and keep refrigerated for up to 6 hours before cooking.

GREMOLATA

PREPARATION TIME: 10 minutes
SERVES 4

1 garlic clove, finely chopped
rind of 1 lemon, pith removed and finely chopped
2 tbsp finely chopped parsley leaves

Put all the ingredients in a small bowl and mix until combined.

JALFREZI CURRY PASTE

PREPARATION TIME: 10 minutes
MAKES enough for 1 recipe quantity of curry

2 garlic cloves, chopped
4cm/1½in piece of root ginger, peeled and chopped
2 tbsp tomato purée
1 tbsp ground coriander
1 tbsp ground cumin
2 tsp tamarind paste
a pinch of cayenne pepper, or to taste

Put the garlic and ginger in a mini food processor and process until a coarse paste forms. Add all of the remaining ingredients and process again, scraping down the side of the bowl as necessary, until blended.

If not using immediately, refrigerate in an airtight container for up to 1 week, or freeze for up to 1 month.

MASSAMAN CURRY PASTE

PREPARATION TIME: 10 minutes
MAKES enough for 1 recipe quantity of curry

1 tbsp tamarind paste
10cm/4in piece of lemongrass stalk, tough outer leaves discarded and finely chopped
1cm/½in piece of root ginger, peeled and finely chopped
2 large garlic cloves, chopped
1 dried red chilli, deseeded if you like, and chopped
1 Thai or small shallot, chopped
2 tsp shrimp paste
1½ tsp ground coriander
1½ tsp ground cumin
1½ tsp fish sauce
½ tsp ground cardamom
½ tsp ground cinnamon
¼ tsp grated nutmeg
a pinch of ground cloves

Put all the ingredients in a mini food processor and process for 1–2 minutes until a thick paste forms, scraping down the side of the bowl as necessary, until well combined.

If not using immediately, refrigerate in an airtight container for up to 1 week, or freeze for up to 1 month.

FINISHING TOUCHES

TOASTED SEEDS & NUTS

COOKING TIME: 1–3 minutes

sesame seeds
pumpkin seeds
pine nuts
flaked almonds

Heat a dry frying pan until hot. Reduce the heat to medium, add the seeds or nuts and dry-fry for 1–2 minutes for sesame seeds, or 2–3 minutes for pumpkin seeds, pine nuts and flaked almonds, until lightly brown. (Shake the pan occasionally to ensure they do not burn.) Remove the pan from the heat and transfer the seeds and nuts to a plate.

ACCOMPANIMENTS

TO SERVE WITH SOUPS

GARLIC CROÛTONS

Don't waste the garlic cloves after they flavour the oil in your pan – they can be added to soups just before puréeing for a real garlic hit, or crush them onto toast.

PREPARATION TIME: 5 minutes
COOKING TIME: 10 minutes
SERVES 4

4 tbsp olive oil, plus extra if needed
4 garlic cloves, peeled
115g/4oz day-old bread, crusts removed and cut into cubes
salt

Heat the oil in a frying pan over a medium-low heat. Add the garlic and fry, stirring, for 3–5 minutes, until lightly browned. Use a slotted spoon to remove the garlic.

Increase the heat to medium, add the bread cubes and fry, turning occasionally, for 3–5 minutes until golden brown and crisp, working in batches to avoid overcrowding the pan and adding extra oil, if necessary. Drain on kitchen paper, then sprinkle with salt.

If not using immediately, leave to cool completely, then store in an airtight container for up to 5 days.

MAPLE CREAM

PREPARATION TIME: 3 minutes
SERVES 4

6 tbsp soured cream
1 tbsp maple syrup, plus extra to taste
a pinch of freshly grated nutmeg, plus extra to taste

Put the soured cream in a small bowl and beat until smooth. Beat in the maple syrup and nutmeg, adding extra to taste, if you like.

If not using immediately, leave to cool completely, then cover and keep refrigerated for up to 4 hours before serving.

PESTO SAUCE

This is best made just before serving, but if you do make it in advance, cover the surface with a thin layer of olive oil to preserve the fresh green colour.

PREPARATION TIME: 10 minutes
SERVES 4

55g/2oz basil leaves
40g/1½oz Parmesan cheese or pecorino cheese, grated
2 garlic cloves, coarsely chopped
1 tbsp pine nuts
125ml/4fl oz/½ cup extra virgin olive oil, plus extra
   if needed
salt and freshly ground black pepper

Put the basil in a mini food processor, sprinkle with salt and process until finely chopped. Add the Parmesan, garlic and pine nuts and process again until finely chopped.

Transfer to a bowl, stir in the olive oil and season with salt and pepper.

If not using immediately, drizzle over a thin layer of olive oil, cover and set aside for up to 4 hours before serving.

TO SERVE WITH MAIN COURSES

ANCHOVY CROÛTES

PREPARATION TIME: 5 minutes
COOKING TIME: 6 minutes
SERVES 4

55g/2oz tinned anchovies in oil
1 garlic clove, finely chopped
2 tbsp finely chopped parsley leaves
¼ tsp smoked or sweet paprika
4 large slices of country bread

Put the anchovies and their oil in a small saucepan over a high heat and stir until the anchovies dissolve into the oil. Stir in the garlic, parsley and paprika, then remove from the heat and set aside.

Meanwhile, preheat the grill to high and position the grill rack 5cm/2in from the heat source. Toast the bread for 2–3 minutes on each side until golden brown and crisp.

Spread the anchovy mixture over each slice of toast, then cut each slice into 3 'fingers'. Serve hot.

CHEESE & MUSTARD CROÛTES

PREPARATION TIME: 5 minutes
COOKING TIME: 7 minutes
SERVES 4

4 slices of sourdough or other bread
4 tbsp wholegrain or Dijon mustard, or to taste
100g/3½oz/scant 1 cup finely grated Gruyère or Cheddar
   cheese
sweet or smoked paprika
vegetarian Worcestershire sauce

Preheat the grill to high and position the grill rack 5cm/2in from the heat source. Toast the bread for 2–3 minutes on each side until golden brown and crisp.

Spread the mustard over each slice of toast, then divide the cheese onto the slices. Sprinkle paprika and a few drops of Worcestershire sauce over the top of each slice.

Return to the grill and grill for about 1 minute until the cheese melts and starts to bubble, then cut each slice into 3 'fingers'. Serve hot.

CUCUMBER & MINT RAITA

PREPARATION TIME: 5 minutes, plus 20 minutes standing
SERVES 4

1 cucumber, deseeded and sliced
4 tbsp thinly sliced mint leaves
250g/9oz/1 cup natural yogurt
salt and freshly ground black pepper

Put the cucumber in a colander, sprinkle with salt and leave to stand in the sink for 20 minutes.

Rinse the cucumber well and pat dry with kitchen paper. Transfer to a bowl, add the mint and yogurt and mix well, then season with pepper.

If not serving immediately, cover and keep refrigerated for up to 4 hours. Just before serving, season with salt and stir.

CUCUMBER & TOMATO RAITA

PREPARATION TIME: 5 minutes, plus 20 minutes standing
SERVES 4

1 cucumber, deseeded and diced
1 red onion, finely chopped
1 large tomato, deseeded and finely chopped
300g/10½oz/1¼ cups natural yogurt
salt and freshly ground black pepper
ground coriander, to serve
ground paprika or cayenne pepper, to serve
finely shredded coriander leaves, to serve

Put the cucumber in a colander, sprinkle with salt and leave to stand in the sink for 20 minutes.

Rinse the cucumber well and pat dry with kitchen paper. Transfer to a bowl, then add the red onion, tomato and yogurt and mix well. Season with pepper.

If not serving immediately, cover and keep refrigerated for up to 4 hours. Just before serving, season with salt and stir, then dust with ground coriander and paprika and sprinkle with coriander leaves.

EGG & PARSLEY SAUCE

PREPARATION TIME: 10 minutes, plus 30 minutes infusing
COOKING TIME: 20 minutes
SERVES 4

400ml/14fl oz/generous 1½ cups milk
½ onion, chopped
3 cloves
1 bay leaf
1½ tsp thyme leaves
a pinch of freshly grated nutmeg, or to taste
2 large eggs, at room temperature
40g/1½oz butter
30g/1oz/¼ cup plain white flour
80ml/2½fl oz/⅓ cup crème fraîche or soured cream
2 tsp anchovy essence
6 tbsp finely chopped parsley leaves
salt and freshly ground black pepper

Put the milk, onion, cloves, bay leaf, thyme and nutmeg in a saucepan and season with pepper. Bring to the boil over a high heat. Remove the pan from the heat, cover and leave to infuse for at least 30 minutes.

Put the eggs in a saucepan. Fill the pan with enough boiling water to cover the eggs by about 2.5cm/1in. Bring to the boil over a high heat, then turn the heat down to low and simmer for 10 minutes. Drain the eggs and set aside until cool enough to handle, then shell and finely chop.

Gently reheat the infused milk and bring to a simmer. Melt the butter in a clean saucepan over a low heat, then add the flour and stir until smooth. Remove the pan from the heat and slowly strain the milk mixture into the flour mixture, a little at a time, stirring until a smooth sauce forms. Discard the solids.

Return the pan to the heat and bring to the boil, then reduce the heat to very low and simmer for 2 minutes.

Stir the eggs into the sauce with the crème fraîche, anchovy essence and parsley. Season with salt and a little more pepper, if you like. Serve hot.

FRIED HALLOUMI

PREPARATION TIME: 5 minutes
COOKING TIME: 5 minutes
SERVES 4

225g/8oz halloumi, drained and thinly sliced
extra virgin olive oil, for frying, plus extra to serve
freshly ground black pepper

Heat a large, heavy-based frying pan over a high heat. Brush the pan with a very thin layer of olive oil and heat until it shimmers.

Reduce the heat to medium-low, add the halloumi and fry for 1–2 minutes until golden brown, working in batches, if necessary. Use a metal spatula to gently turn the cheese over and fry on the other side until golden. Season with pepper. Serve hot, drizzled with extra olive oil.

HORSERADISH & DILL CREAM

PREPARATION TIME: 5 minutes
SERVES 4

150ml/5fl oz/scant ⅔ cup soured cream
1 tbsp freshly grated horseradish, or to taste
1 tbsp dill sprigs, finely chopped
salt

Put the soured cream, horseradish and dill in a small bowl, season with salt and mix well.

If not using immediately, cover and keep refrigerated for up to 10 hours before serving.

PICKLED BEAN SPROUTS

When you first mix the ingredients together, the brine is very salty but it mellows after about half an hour. Don't make these more than two hours in advance or they will lose their crispness.

PREPARATION TIME: 5 minutes, plus cooling and at least 30 minutes chilling
SERVES 4

125ml/4fl oz/½ cup rice vinegar
2 tsp salt

½ tsp grated palm sugar or caster sugar
180g/6¼oz/2 cups bean sprouts, rinsed
1 long, thin red chilli, deseeded and very thinly sliced
1 tbsp very finely snipped chives or shredded spring onion

Put the vinegar, salt and sugar in a small saucepan over a medium heat and stir until the sugar dissolves. Remove the pan from the heat and leave to cool completely.

Transfer the brine to a non-metallic serving bowl and stir in the bean sprouts and chilli, making sure the bean sprouts are coated in the brine.

Cover and chill for at least 30 minutes before serving, but no longer than 2 hours. Serve sprinkled with chives.

SAFFRON RISOTTO

PREPARATION TIME: 10 minutes, plus making the stock (optional)
COOKING TIME: 25 minutes
SERVES 4

1.5l/52fl oz/6 cups Beef Stock (see page 168), Vegetable Stock (see page 169) or ready-made stock
a large pinch of saffron threads
1 tbsp olive oil
30g/1oz butter
1 onion, finely chopped
350g/12oz/scant 1⅔ cups arborio rice
1 tbsp dry white wine
75g/2½oz Parmesan cheese, grated
salt and freshly ground black pepper

Put the stock and saffron in a saucepan over a medium-high heat and bring to just below the boil, then reduce the heat to a simmer.

Meanwhile, heat the oil and half of the butter in a frying pan over a medium heat. Add the onion and fry, stirring, for 3–5 minutes until softened. Add the rice and stir until coated. Add the wine and leave it to bubble until it evaporates.

Add the simmering stock one ladleful at a time, stirring continuously and making sure the rice has absorbed the liquid before adding more. Continue until all the liquid has been absorbed, until all the stock has been used and the rice is tender but still retains a slight bite. This will take about 20 minutes.

Remove the pan from the heat, stir in the Parmesan and the remaining butter and season with salt and pepper. Serve hot.

SALSA VERDE

The salsa verde can be made in advance and chilled until required, but it is best made just before serving so the vibrant green colour doesn't dull.

PREPARATION TIME: 5 minutes
SERVES 4

8 anchovy fillets in oil, drained and chopped
2–4 large garlic cloves, chopped
1 tbsp capers in brine, rinsed
250ml/9fl oz/1 cup extra virgin olive oil
1 large handful of basil leaves
1 large handful of parsley leaves

Put the anchovies, garlic, capers and 2 tablespoons of the olive oil in a mini food processor and process until chopped but not puréed.

Add the basil and parsley and process again until finely chopped, then transfer to a serving bowl and stir in the remaining olive oil.

If not using immediately, cover and keep refrigerated for up to 1 day before serving.

TORTILLA CHIPS

If you don't have a deep frying pan, cut each of the longest tortilla strips in half again. This is because the longer the strips are, the more they curl and they won't cook all the way through if they are not flat.

PREPARATION TIME: 15 minutes
COOKING TIME: 12 minutes
SERVES 4

sunflower oil, for frying
4 corn tortillas, 15cm/6in each, cut into 1cm/½in strips
ancho chilli powder or cayenne pepper, for sprinkling
salt and freshly ground black pepper

Line a plate with kitchen paper and set aside. Heat a 5cm/2in layer of oil in a deep frying pan over a medium-high heat until very hot. To test if the oil is hot enough, drop a piece of tortilla into the oil – it should sizzle immediately.

Working in batches, add the tortilla strips and deep-fry, stirring, for 2–3 minutes until golden brown and crisp. Use a slotted spoon to remove the chips from the pan and drain on the paper-lined plate. Season with salt and pepper and sprinkle with chilli powder. Leave to cool completely, then toss until evenly coated in the seasonings.

If not serving immediately, store in an airtight container for up to 2 days.

WATERCRESS SAUCE

PREPARATION TIME: 5 minutes
COOKING TIME: 5 minues
SERVES 4

55g/2oz watercress, any thick stalks removed
2 tbsp chopped chervil
2 tbsp chopped dill
2 tbsp finely chopped parsley leaves
¼ tsp lemon juice, or to taste
180ml/6fl oz/¾ cup crème fraîche or soured cream
salt and freshly ground black pepper

Bring a small saucepan of unsalted water to the boil. Add the watercress and blanch for 30 seconds, then immediately drain and refresh under cold running water. Squeeze to remove as much water as possible.

Put the watercress, chervil, dill and parsley in a mini food processor and process until finely chopped.

Transfer to a bowl, stir in the lemon juice and crème fraîche and season with salt and pepper.

If not using immediately, cover and leave to one side for up to 4 hours before serving.

TO SERVE WITH DESSERTS

BRANDY BUTTER

PREPARATION TIME: 5 minutes
SERVES 4

85g/3oz butter, softened
85g/3oz/⅓ cup caster sugar
1 tbsp milk
1 tbsp brandy
85g/3oz/⅔ cup icing sugar, sifted

Put the butter in a bowl and beat until light and fluffy. Beat in the sugar, milk and brandy, then sift in the icing sugar. Continue beating until well combined and the butter is light and fluffy.

If not using immediately, cover and keep refrigerated for up to 2 days or freeze for up to 2 months.

BUTTERSCOTCH SAUCE

PREPARATION TIME: 5 minutes
COOKING TIME: 5 minutes
SERVES 4

175g/6oz/¾ cup caster sugar
60g/2¼oz butter
125ml/4fl oz/½ cup double cream

Put the sugar and 4 tablespoons water in a saucepan over a medium heat and stir until the sugar dissolves.

Increase the heat to high and boil, without stirring, until the caramel turns a dark golden brown colour. Watch closely because it can burn quickly. Immediately remove the pan from the heat, add the butter and whisk it in, then whisk in the cream. Serve hot.

DARK TOFFEE SAUCE

PREPARATION TIME: 10 minutes
COOKING TIME: 10 minutes
SERVES 4

75g/2½oz butter, diced
150g/5½oz/heaped ¾ cup dark muscovado sugar
150ml/5fl oz/scant ⅔ cup double cream
1 tsp vanilla extract

Melt the butter in a saucepan over a medium heat. Add the sugar, cream and vanilla extract and stir until the sugar dissolves, then bring to the boil. Immediately reduce the heat to low and simmer for 5 minutes until the sauce thickens. Serve hot.

FRESH ORANGE SAUCE

PREPARATION TIME: 10 minutes
COOKING TIME: 5 minutes
SERVES 4

1½ tsp arrowroot or cornflour
1 tbsp caster sugar
finely grated zest of 1 large orange
150ml/5fl oz/scant ⅔ cup freshly squeezed orange juice
1 tsp butter
2 tsp orange-flavoured liqueur (optional)

Put the arrowroot, sugar and orange zest in a heatproof bowl and stir together. Add 2 tablespoons of the orange juice and stir until smooth.

Put the remaining orange juice in a saucepan and bring to the boil over a high heat, then beat it into the arrowroot mixture until smooth.

Return the mixture to the pan and return to the boil, stirring until the sauce is thick and clear. Beat in the butter, then stir in the liqueur, if using. Serve hot.

HOT CHOCOLATE SAUCE

PREPARATION TIME: 5 minutes, plus 30 minutes preheating the cooker
COOKING TIME: 15 minutes on HIGH
SERVES 4

75g/2½oz butter, diced
75g/2½oz dark chocolate, 70% cocoa solids, finely chopped
2 tbsp caster sugar
⅛ tsp vanilla extract
a pinch of salt

Preheat the covered slow cooker on HIGH for 30 minutes.

Put all of the ingredients in the cooker, then pour over 3 tablespoons boiling water and stir until the chocolate has completely dissolved.

Cover the cooker and cook on HIGH for 15 minutes. Serve the sauce hot, or leave on the WARM setting until required.

INDEX